It's another Quality Book from CGP

This book is for anyone doing AQA A GCSE Geography at Higher Level.

It contains lots of tricky exam-style questions designed to make you sweat — because that's the only way you'll get any better.

There are questions to see what you know. There are questions to test your geographical skills. And it's jam-packed with hints and tips — so you'll be well prepared for your exams.

We've also put some daft bits in to try and make the whole experience at least vaguely entertaining for you.

What CGP is all about

Our sole aim here at CGP is to produce the highest quality books — carefully written, immaculately presented and dangerously close to being funny.

Then we work our socks off to get them out to you — at the cheapest possible prices.

Physical Geography

Contents

Getting Started
Exam Breakdown and Answering Questions 1
Answering Questions 2

Unit 1A — The Restless Earth
Tectonic Plates 3
Fold Mountains 4
Volcanoes 5
Supervolcanoes 7
Earthquakes 8
Tsunamis 10

Unit 1A — Rocks, Resources and Scenery
Types of Rock 11
The Rock Cycle 12
Weathering 13
Rocks and Landscapes 14
Using Landscapes 16
Quarrying Impacts 18
Quarrying Management 19

Unit 1A — Weather and Climate
UK Climate 20
Depressions and Anticyclones 22
Extreme UK Weather 23
Global Climate Change — Debate 24
Global Climate Change — Impacts 25
Global Climate Change — Responses 26
Tropical Storms 27

Unit 1A — The Living World
Ecosystems 28
World Ecosystems 29
Temperate Deciduous Forest 32
Tropical Rainforest — Deforestation 33
Tropical Rainforest — Sustainable Management ... 34
Hot Deserts 36

Unit 1B — Water on the Land
The River Valley 37
Erosion, Transportation and Deposition 38
River Landforms 39
River Discharge 42
Flooding 43
Hard vs Soft Engineering 44
Managing the UK's Water 45

Unit 1B — Ice on the Land
Ice Levels Over Time 46
Glacial Budget 47
Glacial Erosion 48
Glacial Transport and Deposition 50
Impacts and Management of Tourism on Ice 51
Impacts of Glacial Retreat 52

Unit 1B — The Coastal Zone *(Physical Geography)*

- Coastal Weathering and Erosion 53
- Coastal Landforms Caused by Erosion 54
- Coastal Transportation and Deposition 56
- Coastal Landforms Caused by Deposition............. 57
- Rising Sea Level and Coastal Flooding 58
- Coastal Erosion.. 59
- Coastal Management Strategies 60
- Coastal Habitat 61

Unit 2A — Population Change *(Human Geography)*

- Population Growth 62
- Population Growth and Structure 63
- Managing Rapid Population Growth 64
- Managing Ageing Populations 65
- Population Movements.. 67
- Migration Within and To the EU 68

Unit 2A — Changing Urban Environments

- Urbanisation 69
- Parts of a City 70
- Urban Issues 71
- Squatter Settlements.. 73
- Urbanisation — Environmental Issues 75
- Sustainable Cities 76

Unit 2A — Changing Rural Environments

- Change in the Rural-Urban Fringe 77
- Change in Rural Areas 78
- Change in UK Commercial Farming 79
- Sustainable Rural Living 81
- Changes to Farming in Tropical Areas 82
- Factors Affecting Farming in Tropical Areas 84

Unit 2B — The Development Gap

- Measuring Development 85
- Global Inequalities 86
- Causes of Global Inequalities 87
- Reducing Global Inequality 90
- Inequalities in the EU 93

Unit 2B — Globalisation

- Globalisation Basics 94
- Trans-National Corporations (TNCs) 95
- Change in Manufacturing Location 96
- Globalisation and Energy Demand 97
- Globalisation and Food Supply 98
- Reducing the Impacts of Globalisation 99

Unit 2B — Tourism

- Growth in Tourism 102
- UK Tourism 103
- Mass Tourism 106
- Tourism in Extreme Environments 107
- Ecotourism 108

Published by CGP

Editors:
Ellen Bowness, Katie Braid, Joe Brazier, Ben Fletcher, Rosie Gillham, Murray Hamilton, Jane Towle, Karen Wells.

Contributor:
Helen Nurton.

Proofreading:
Julie Wakeling, Eileen Worthington.

ISBN: 978 1 84762 379 9

With thanks to Laura Jakubowski for copyright research.

Graph of tiltmeter readings at Mount St Helens on page 6 © Earth Science Australia 1995-2009. www.earthsci.org

Data used to construct the graph of sulfur dioxide emissions at Mount St Helens on page 6 © U.S. Geological Survey, www.usgs.gov

Map of Mount St Helens on page 7 © Steven Dutch, University of Wisconsin-Green Bay

Map of Yellowstone National Park on page 7 © U.S. Geological Survey, www.usgs.gov

Data used to compile the graph on page 7 and the map on page 10 © U.S. Geological Survey, www.usgs.gov

Map of UK geology on page 11 reproduced by kind permission of the British Geological Survey. ©NERC. All rights reserved. IPR/119-11CT.

With thanks to Science Photo Library for permission to reproduce the photograph on page 13.

With thanks to iStockphoto.com for permission to reproduce the photographs used on pages 14, 15, 28, 39, 41, 48, 55, 73, 84 and 88.

Graphs on pages 20, 21 and 24 adapted from Crown Copyright data supplied by the Met Office.

Data used to compile the graph on page 25 adapted from Climate Change 2001: The Scientific Basis. Contribution of Working Group I to the Third Assessment Report of the Intergovernmental Panel on Climate Change. Figure 5. Cambridge University Press

Data used to compile the table on page 26, source: http://www.direct.gov.uk/en/Motoring/OwningAVehicle/HowToTaxYourVehicle/DG_10012524 © Crown copyright

Mapping data on pages 40, 49 and 57 reproduced by permission of Ordnance Survey® on behalf of HMSO © Crown copyright (2009). All rights reserved. Ordnance Survey® Licence No. 100034841.

Data used to compile the UK average rainfall map on page 45 from the Manchester Metropolitan University.

Data used to compile the UK population density map on page 45 from Office for National Statistics: General Register Office for Scotland, Northern Ireland Statistics & Research Agency. © Crown copyright reproduced under the terms of the Click-Use Licence.

Data used to construct the flow map on page 67, source: International Passenger Survey, Office for National Statistics © Crown copyright reproduced under the terms of the Click-Use Licence

Data used to compile the table on page 68 © Reuters Foundation 2002

Data used to compile the table on page 85 (except GNI per capita data) and table on page 86 © Central Intelligence Agency

Data used to compile the table on page 87 and the graph on page 89 from Human Development report 2009 © United Nations 2009. Reproduced with permission.

Data used to compile the graph on page 87 © United Nations, 2009. Reproduced with permission.

Data use to compile the pie charts on page 88 © World Trade Organisation, http://stat.wto.org/CountryProfile/WSDBCountryPFView.aspx?Language=E&Country=AU,BE,CA,CN,TH,UG,GB,UY,ZM,NI

Information used to compile the article on page 90 © www.kibera.net

Data use to compile the map on page 91 © www.ustr.gov

Data used to compile the article on page 92 from DFID, 'Working to reduce poverty in Ghana' © Crown copyright

Data used to compile the map on page 93 © European Communities, 1995-2009

Data used to compile the graph on page 94 © Crown copyright, reproduced under the terms of the Click-Use Licence.

Data used to compile the graph on page 97, sources: History: Energy Information Administration (EIA), 'International Energy Annual 2006' (June-December 2008). Projections: EIA, 'World Energy Projections Plus' (2009).

Data used to compile the graph on page 100 © Crown copyright, reproduced under the terms of the Click-Use Licence.

Data used to compile the UK tourism graphs on pages 102 and 103 from Office for National Statistics: General Register Office for Scotland, Northern Ireland Statistics & Research Agency. © Crown copyright reproduced under the terms of the Click-Use Licence.

Groovy website: www.cgpbooks.co.uk
Printed by Elanders Ltd, Newcastle upon Tyne.
Jolly bits of clipart from CorelDRAW®

Based on the classic CGP style created by Richard Parsons.

Psst... photocopying this Workbook isn't allowed, even if you've got a CLA licence. Luckily, it's dead cheap, easy and quick to order more copies from CGP — just call us on 0870 750 1242. Phew!

Text, design, layout and original illustrations © Coordination Group Publications Ltd. (CGP) 2010
All rights reserved.

Getting Started

Exam Breakdown and Answering Questions

Welcome to the wonderful world of exam practice. This book will help you get a bit of practice at the kind of questions they're going to throw at you in the exam. It'll also help you to figure out what you need to revise — practise the questions for the topics you've learnt in class and if there are any questions that you can't answer then go back and revise that topic some more.

There are Two Exams For GCSE Geography

First up, here's what you've got to do — we'll come on to how to do it in a bit. You'll have to sit two exams for GCSE Geography — one for Unit 1 (Physical Geography) and one for Unit 2 (Human Geography).

Unit 1 Exam: Physical Geography

Here's how it's structured:

1 hour 30 minutes	75 marks in total	37.5% of your final mark

- There are seven questions in total.
- You need to answer three out of the seven questions — one question from Section A, one question from Section B, then a third question from either section.

Unit 2 Exam: Human Geography

Here's how it's structured:

1 hour 30 minutes	84 marks in total	37.5% of your final mark

- There are six questions in total.
- You need to answer three out of the six questions — one question from Section A, one question from Section B, then a third question from either section.

You get marks for spelling, punctuation and grammar in Unit 2 — that's why it's worth more marks than Unit 1.

Pick Your Questions Carefully in the Exam

1) If you've only studied three topics in class for Unit 1 then it's pretty obvious that you need to answer the exam questions on those three topics.
2) But, if you've studied more than three you've got a bit of choice in the exam. Have a quick look at ALL the questions on the topics you've studied and figure out which ones are easiest — look at all the parts though (don't just go for one where you can answer the first part and none of the rest).

Make Sure you Understand what the Question's Asking You to Do

It's dead easy to misread a question and spend five minutes writing about the wrong thing. Four simple tips can help you avoid this:

1) Figure out if it's a case study question — if the question wording includes 'using named examples' or 'with reference to one named area' you need to include a case study.
2) Underline the command words in the question (the ones that tell you what to do).
3) Underline the key words (the ones that tell you what it's about), e.g. volcanoes, tourism, immigrants.
4) Re-read the question and your answer when you've finished, just to check that what you've written really does answer the question being asked. A common mistake is to miss a bit out — like when questions say 'use data from the graph in your answer' or 'use evidence from the map'.

Command word	Means write about...
Describe	what it's like
Explain	why it's like that (i.e. give reasons)
Compare	the similarities AND differences
Contrast	the differences
Suggest why	give reasons for

Getting Started

Answering Questions

Some Questions are Level Marked

1) For some questions you'll get marks for writing specific words or sentences — each correct one you give will be worth 1 mark, up to a maximum of four marks.
2) Other questions are level marked — your answer will be judged to be basic (level 1), clear (level 2) or detailed (level 3). The higher the level of your answer, the more marks you'll get.
3) Here's a bit about what's expected from different level answers:

Level 1 answers...	Level 2 answers...	Level 3 answers...
...show you have basic knowledge and understanding of the topic. You won't have used many specialist terms (geographical words), your ideas won't be linked together and your answer won't have much structure.	...show you have good knowledge and clear understanding of the topic. You'll have used some specialist terms, structured your answer well and linked some of your ideas together.	...show you have detailed knowledge and understanding of the topic. You'll have used evidence and examples to support your points and will have spotted links between different points. You'll have used a range of specialist terms and will have structured your answer really well.

4) Level marked questions are worth 4, 6 or 8 marks. In 4 and 6 mark questions you only need to reach level 2 to get full marks. To get top marks on 8 mark questions (usually case study questions) you'll need to deliver a super duper level 3 answer.
5) For case study questions, it's a good idea to write a mini plan of how you're going to answer the question, e.g. if the question is 'Describe the cause and impacts of a volcanic eruption you have studied' your plan might be:
6) Make sure you INCLUDE PLENTY OF DETAILS, e.g. place names, facts, dates etc.
7) For Unit 2 (human geography), each of the 8 mark questions also has another 3 marks available for spelling, punctuation and grammar. To get top marks you need to:

Level marked questions don't have one right answer, so you won't find full written answers for them in the answer book. Instead, there are 'hints' telling you the types of thing you need to write to get top marks.

- name of volcano, where it is, when it erupted
- the cause of the eruption
- primary impacts
- secondary impacts

- Make sure your spelling, punctuation and grammar is consistently correct.
- Write in a way that makes it clear what you mean.
- Use a wide range of geographical terms (e.g. sustainable development) correctly.

Here are a Few Other Handy Hints to Remember...

1) Take a calculator into the exam — you may need to work things out that you can't do in your head.
2) A ruler and protractor are also essential for reading and drawing graphs.
3) Draw any diagrams in pencil, that way if you get something wrong you can rub it out (which reminds me... don't forget to take a rubber in too).
4) Use the number of marks each part of a question is worth to figure out how much time to spend on it — for every one mark you've got a little bit over one minute, e.g. if it's a 4 mark question you've got 5 minutes to answer it.
5) Do the questions that you know the answers to first and leave the trickier ones till later.
6) If you're running out of time at the end of the exam don't panic — just write what you can as bullet points. You'll still get some marks for doing this.

Getting Started

Unit 1A — The Restless Earth

Tectonic Plates

1 Study **Figure 1**, which shows the Earth's tectonic plates.

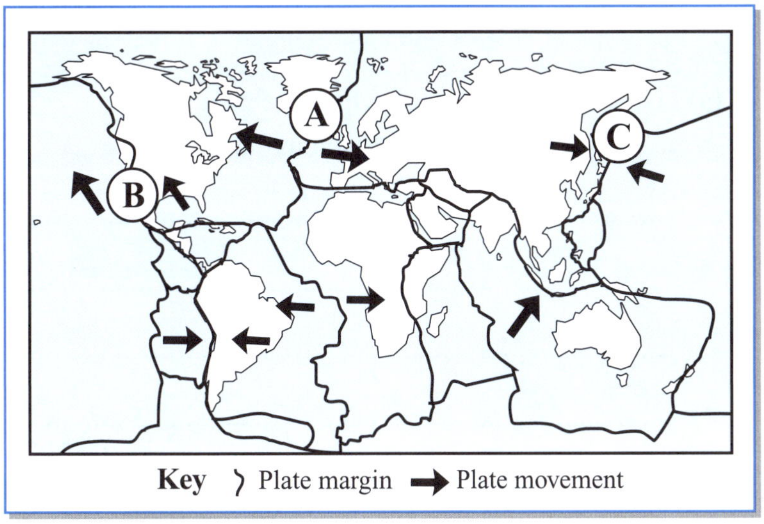

(a) Name the type of plate margin labelled A in **Figure 1** and explain why new crust forms there.

....

....

(3 marks)

(b) The San Andreas Fault is labelled B in **Figure 1**.
Crust is neither formed or destroyed at this plate margin.
What is this type of plate margin called?

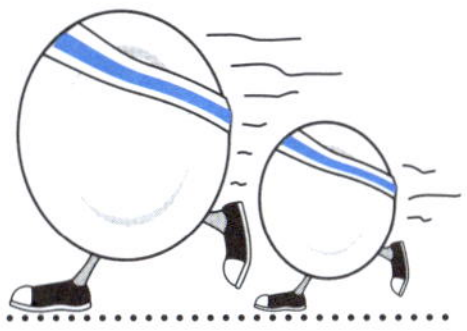

....

(1 mark)

(c) At the plate margin labelled C in **Figure 1**, continental crust meets oceanic crust.
Describe how continental crust is different from oceanic crust.

....

....

(2 marks)

Figure 2

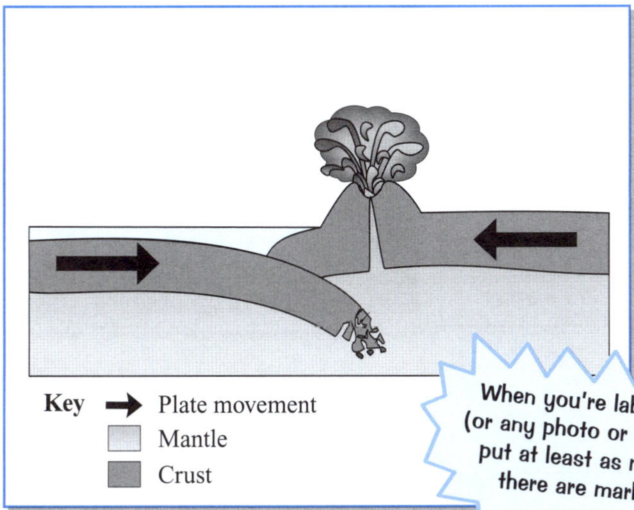

(d) **Figure 2** is a diagram of a plate margin.

  (i) What type of plate margin does it show?

  ....

  (1 mark)

  (ii) Label the types of plates and the features that form at the margin.

  (4 marks)

When you're labelling a sketch (or any photo or diagram) always put at least as many labels as there are marks available.

Fold Mountains

1   Study **Figure 1**, which is a map of a fold mountain area.

Figure 1

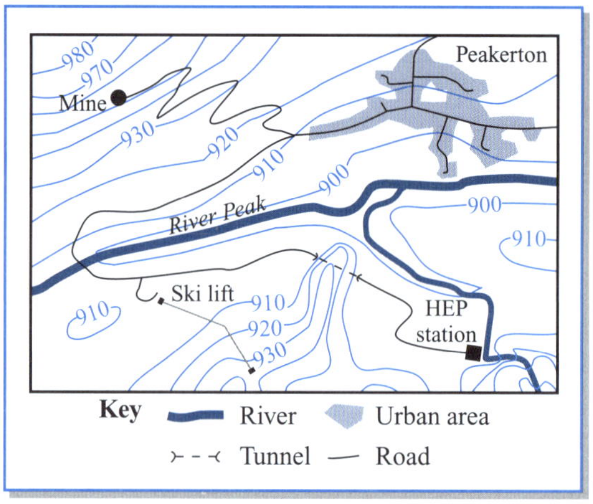

(a) (i)   State the ways in which the area shown in **Figure 1** is being used.

    ....
    ....
    ....
    ....
    (3 marks)

   (ii) Describe, using evidence from **Figure 1**, how people have adapted to living in the area.

    ....
    ....
    (2 marks)

(b) (i)   At which type of plate margin can fold mountains be found?

    ....
    (1 mark)

   (ii) Describe how fold mountains are formed.

    ....
    ....
    (2 marks)

(c) Study **Figure 2**, which shows the Rockies in North America. The Rockies are a fold mountain area. Describe the characteristics of fold mountain areas.

    Figure 2

    Use the photo to help you — say what characteristics you see.

    ....
    ....
    ....
    ....
    (3 marks)

(d) Describe the ways in which a fold mountain area you have studied is used.

    (8 marks)

(e) Describe how people have adapted to the conditions in a fold mountain area you have studied.

    The wording 'you have studied' tells you it's a case study question.

    (8 marks)

Unit 1A — The Restless Earth

Volcanoes

1   Study **Figure 1**, which shows the Earth's tectonic plates and the distribution of volcanoes.

Figure 1

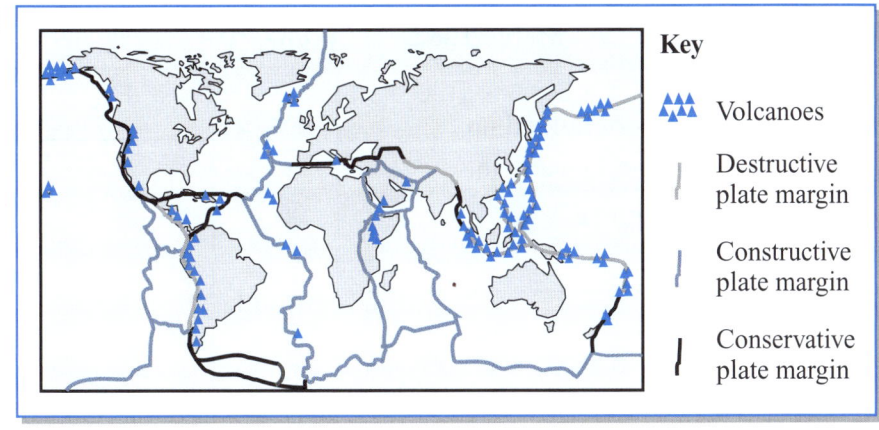

Key:
- Volcanoes
- Destructive plate margin
- Constructive plate margin
- Conservative plate margin

(a) Describe and explain the global distribution of volcanoes.

When describing the distribution of something talk about the general pattern and any anomalies.

....

....

....

....

....
(6 marks)

(b) Study **Figure 2**, which shows a cross-section through a shield volcano.

Figure 2

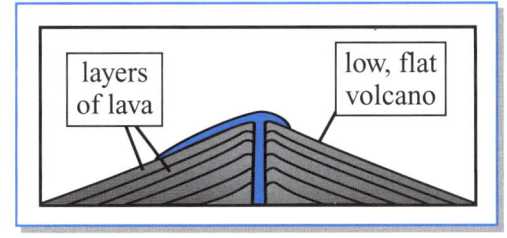

- layers of lava
- low, flat volcano

(i) Explain how the volcano gets its characteristic shape.

....

....

....
(2 marks)

(ii) Contrast the characteristics of shield volcanoes and composite volcanoes.

'Contrast' means write about the differences.

....

....

....

....

....
(4 marks)

(c) For a volcanic eruption you have studied, describe the cause and the primary and secondary impacts.

(8 marks)

Unit 1A — The Restless Earth

Volcanoes

2 Study **Figure 3**, which shows measurements made by scientists on Mount St. Helens in the USA, before a minor eruption on the 19th March 1982.

Figure 3

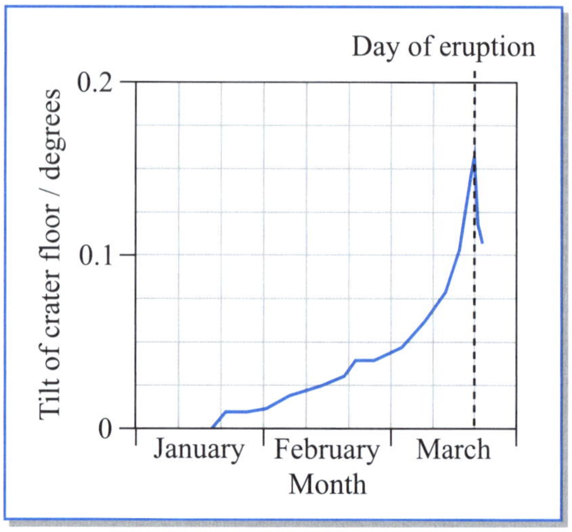

(a) (i) Suggest why the crater floor bulged up before the volcano erupted, causing the increased tilt shown in **Figure 3**.

....
....
(1 mark)

(ii) Describe what happened to the tilt of the crater floor after the eruption, and suggest why.

....
....
(2 marks)

Figure 4

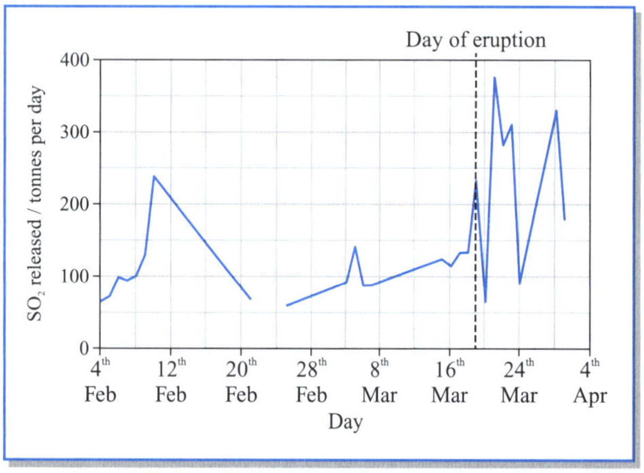

(b) Study **Figure 4**, which shows measurements of sulfur dioxide emissions made on Mount St. Helens.

(i) How much sulfur dioxide was released on the day of the eruption?

....
(1 mark)

Draw your own lines on graphs in the exam to help you read them.

(ii) Complete **Figure 4** to show that 100 tonnes of sulfur dioxide were released on 24th February.
(1 mark)

(c) Which measurement (the tilt of the crater floor or the release of sulfur dioxide) gave a better warning of when the volcano was going to erupt? Explain your answer.

....
....
(2 marks)

(d) Suggest one other way that scientists could monitor a volcano to predict when it will erupt.

....
(1 mark)

(e) For a named volcanic eruption, describe the immediate and long-term responses to the eruption.
(8 marks)

Unit 1A — The Restless Earth

Supervolcanoes

1 Study **Figure 1**, which shows contour maps of Mount St. Helens (a volcano) and Yellowstone National Park (a supervolcano).

(a) Using evidence from **Figure 1**, compare the characteristics of volcanoes and supervolcanoes.

....

....

....

....

....

Watch out for differences in scale when you're comparing maps.

Figure 1

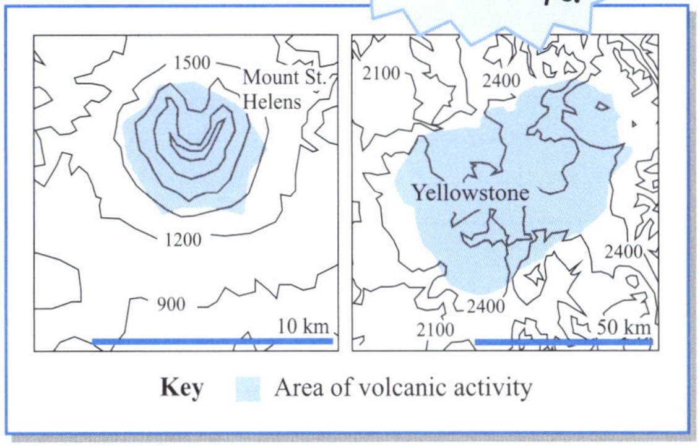

'Using evidence from Figure 1' means you need to refer to the figure in your answer.

(6 marks)

(b) Briefly describe how supervolcanoes form at hotspots.

....

....

....

(4 marks)

(c) **Figure 2** shows the volume of lava that erupted from some volcanoes and supervolcanoes.

Figure 2

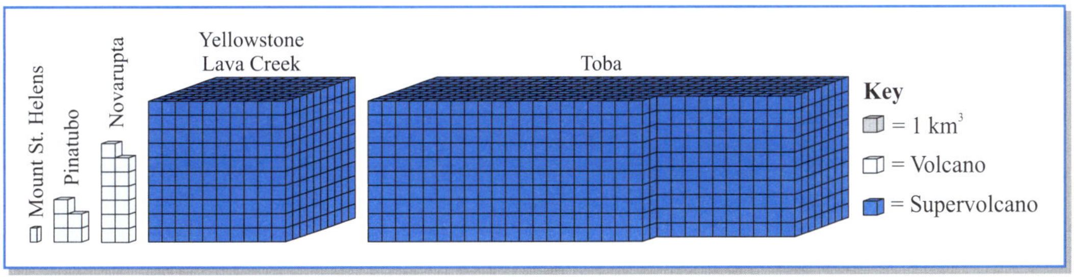

Key: ▢ = 1 km^3, ▢ = Volcano, ▢ = Supervolcano

Don't forget to include the units.

(i) How much lava erupted from Novarupta? ....

(1 mark)

(ii) Using **Figure 2**, compare the volume of lava ejected by volcanoes and supervolcanoes.

....

....

(2 marks)

(iii) Suggest one other way in which the effects of supervolcanoes are different from volcanoes.

....

....

(2 marks)

Unit 1A — The Restless Earth

Earthquakes

1 Study **Figure 1**, which shows the Earth's tectonic plates and the distribution of earthquakes.

(a) Describe the distribution of earthquakes around the world.

Figure 1

....

....

....

....

....

(2 marks)

Key ⋰ Earthquakes | Plate margin

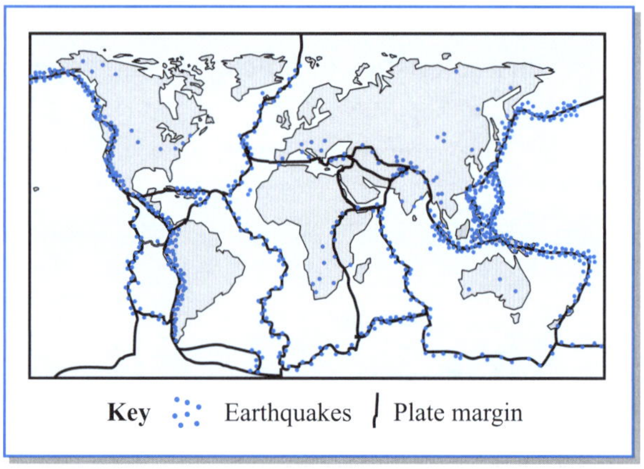

(b) Explain how earthquakes are caused at destructive plate margins.

....

....

> Make sure you use geographical words in your answer, e.g. shockwaves.

....

....

(4 marks)

2 Study **Figure 2**, which shows the focus of the 1994 Northridge earthquake in California, USA.

Figure 2

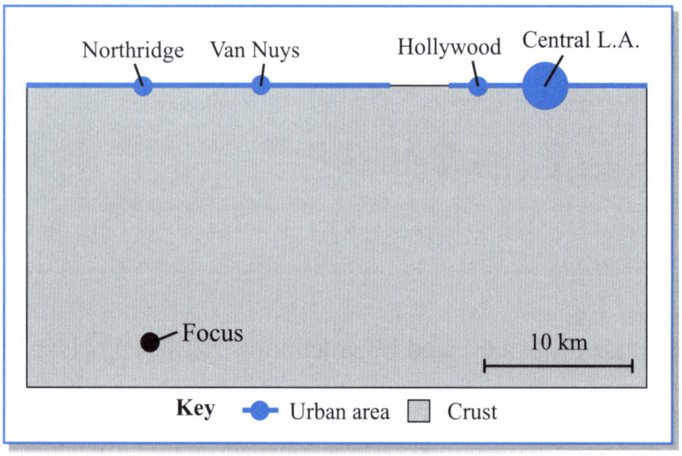

Northridge Van Nuys Hollywood Central L.A.

• Focus

10 km

Key — Urban area ▢ Crust

(a) (i) Define the term 'focus'.

....

....

....

(1 mark)

(ii) How deep in the Earth was the focus of this earthquake?

....

(1 mark)

> Use the scale and a ruler to answer this question.

(b) Label the epicentre of the earthquake on **Figure 2**.

(1 mark)

(c) Shockwaves from the earthquake caused damage up to 125 km away. What are shockwaves?

....

(1 mark)

Unit 1A — The Restless Earth

Earthquakes

3 In 2008 there was an earthquake in Sichuan, China, that measured 7.9 on the Richter scale.

(a) (i) Describe how earthquakes are measured using the Richter scale.

....

....
(2 marks)

(ii) The Richter scale is logarithmic. How much more powerful is an earthquake with a magnitude of 8 compared to an earthquake with a magnitude of 7?

....
(1 mark)

(b) (i) Study **Figure 3**, which shows how the Richter scale relates to the Mercalli scale. Describe the damage you would have expected to see after the earthquake in Sichuan.

....

....

....
(1 mark)

(ii) How is the Mercalli scale measured?

....

....

....
(1 mark)

Figure 3

The Richter scale	The Mercalli scale
1	1 Only detected by instruments
	2 Only felt by people at rest indoors
2	3 Felt by people indoors
3	4 Felt by many people, dishes and windows rattle
	5 Felt by most people, dishes and windows broken
4	6 Felt by everyone, many objects moved
5	7 Some structural damage
6	8 Heavy structural damage
7	9 Massive structural damage, some buildings destroyed
8	10 All buildings damaged, many destroyed
	11 Most buildings destroyed
9+	12 Total destruction

(c) Describe and compare the primary impacts of earthquakes in rich and poor parts of the world that you have studied.

(8 marks)

> Make sure you describe AND compare — you have to do both to get top marks.

4 Describe and compare the preparation and immediate responses to earthquakes in rich and poor parts of the world that you have studied.

(8 marks)

Unit 1A — The Restless Earth

Tsunamis

1   **Figure 1** is a newspaper extract describing a tsunami that hit Papua New Guinea in 1998.

Figure 1

Tsunami Devastates Papua New Guinea
Over 2000 people estimated killed
Thousands homeless as villages destroyed

The coast of Papua New Guinea was hit by waves over 10 metres high on Friday evening. A string of villages along a thin strip of land between Sissano Lagoon and the Pacific Ocean were completely flattened. The tsunami was thought to be caused by a huge underwater landslide triggered by a magnitude 7.1 earthquake. The tsunami drowned many people and destroyed houses, schools and fishing boats. It also felled a large number of coconut trees along the coastline. Surviving families have fled inland, unwilling to return to the sea to fish and fearing the spread of disease. Rescue workers fear that the water could be contaminated for months to come.

(a) Using **Figure 1**, describe one economic impact and one environmental impact of the tsunami.

....

....
(2 marks)

(b) Study **Figure 2**, which shows the locations hit by the tsunami and the height of the waves at that place. Coastal villages between Arnold River and Malol were heavily damaged by waves.

Figure 2

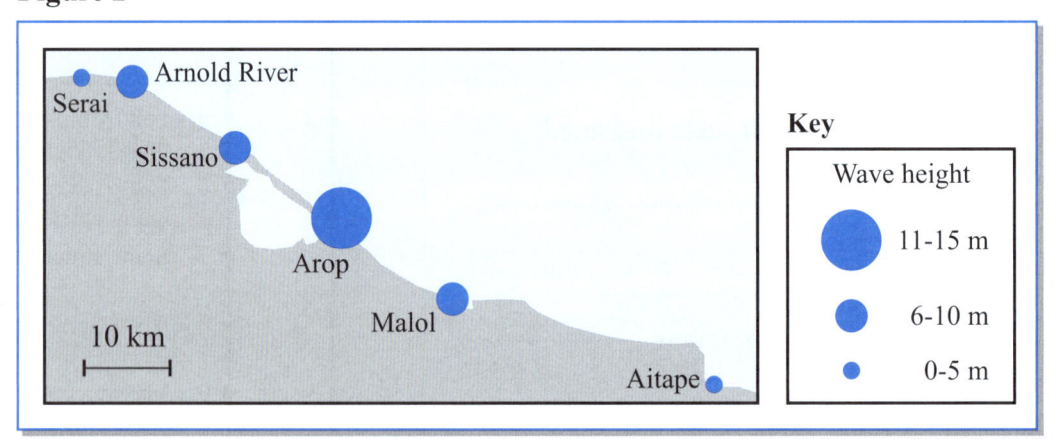

(i) What length of coastline was hit by waves high enough to heavily damage villages?

....
(1 mark)

(ii) How high did waves have to be to heavily damage villages?..
(1 mark)

(iii) Which area was hit by the tallest waves?..
(1 mark)

(c) Describe the cause and effects of a tsunami you have studied.
(8 marks)

(d) Describe the responses to a tsunami you have studied.
(8 marks)

Unit 1A — The Restless Earth

Unit 1A — Rocks, Resources and Scenery

Types of Rock

1   Study **Figure 1**, which shows the distribution of the three rock types in the UK.

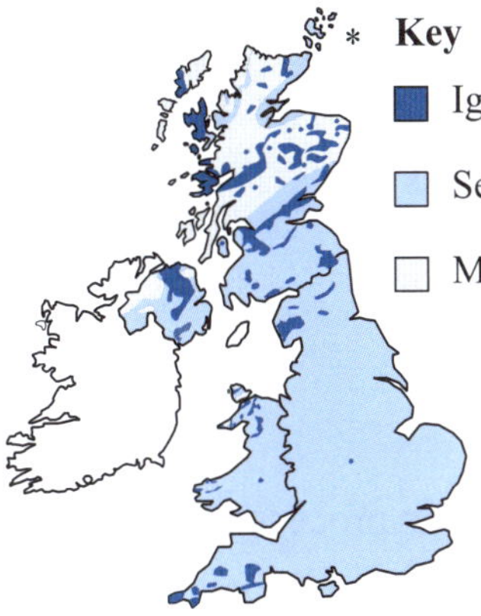

(a) (i) Use **Figure 1** to identify the most common rock type in the UK.

....
(1 mark)

Figure 1

Key
- Igneous rocks
- Sedimentary rocks
- Metamorphic rocks

(ii) Give an example of this rock type and describe how it's formed.

....
....
....
....
....
(3 marks)

(iii) Use **Figure 1** to identify the least common rock type in the UK and describe its distribution.

....

To describe the distribution of something you just have to talk about where it's found.

....
....
....
....
(4 marks)

(b) (i) Describe how igneous rocks are formed.

....
(1 mark)

(ii) Explain why the texture of intrusive igneous rock is different from the texture of extrusive igneous rock.

....
....
....
....
(4 marks)

The Rock Cycle

1 Study **Figure 1**, which shows the rock cycle.

(a) (i) Process A acting on magma creates rock type B. Name the process labelled A and the rock type labelled B in **Figure 1**.

A: ....

B: ....

(2 marks)

Figure 1

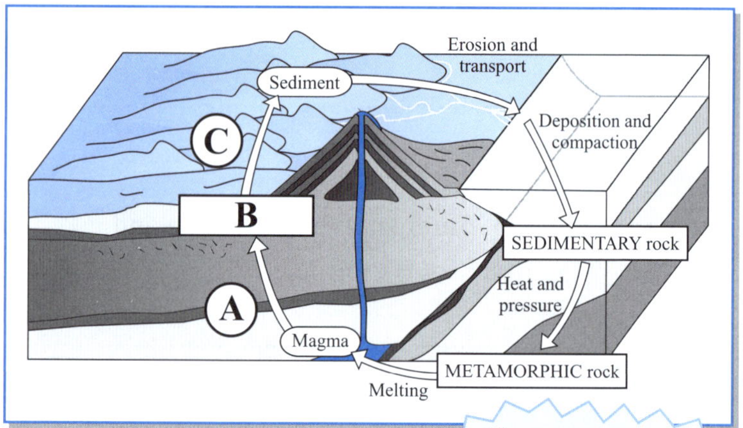

(ii) Name the process labelled C in **Figure 1** and explain why it's important to the rock cycle.

....

....

....

(2 marks)

(iii) Using **Figure 1**, describe the formation of metamorphic rocks.

....

(1 mark)

Figure 2

Geological period	Began, million years before present
Quaternary	2.6
Tertiary	65
Cretaceous	145
Jurassic	215
Triassic	245
Permian	285
Carboniferous	360
Devonian	410
Silurian	440
Ordovician	505
Cambrian	585

Even if you don't know the right answers it's worth guessing — you won't lose any marks.

(b) **Figure 2** shows the most recent geological time periods.

(i) How much time passed between the beginning of the Carboniferous and the Cretaceous period?

....

(1 mark)

(ii) Using **Figure 2**, state the geological period that the following four rocks were formed in across the UK:

Granite, Clay, Chalk, Carboniferous limestone

....

....

....

....

(4 marks)

Unit 1A — Rocks, Resources and Scenery

Weathering

1 **Figure 1** shows some weathered rocks in a dry desert.

Figure 1

(a) (i) Describe the type of mechanical weathering that's likely to have affected the rocks in **Figure 1**.

....
....
....
....
....
(4 marks)

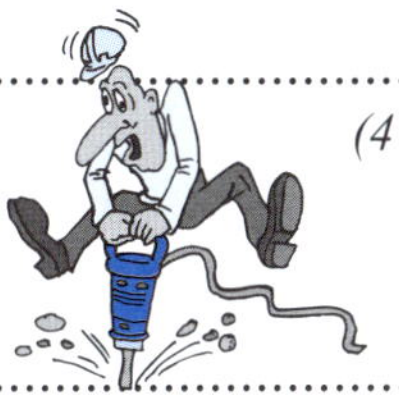

Read the question introduction carefully — it could help you to get the right answer.

(ii) Name another type of mechanical weathering.

....
(1 mark)

(b) (i) Contrast chemical weathering with mechanical weathering.

....
....
(2 marks)

(ii) Describe the process of carbonation weathering.

....
....
(2 marks)

(iii) Name another type of chemical weathering.

....
(1 mark)

(c) How are rocks broken down by biological weathering?

When you're asked about how a process works you should always describe what it is first.

....
....
....
....
(3 marks)

Unit 1A — Rocks, Resources and Scenery

Rocks and Landscapes

1   Study **Figure 1**, which is a photograph of a landscape.

   (a) (i) What type of rock is the landscape in **Figure 1** based on?

   Figure 1

   ....
   (1 mark)

   (ii) Label **Figure 1** to show the characteristics of the landscape.
   (3 marks)

   (b) Describe how the features of the rock shown in **Figure 1** result in the formation of tors.

   ....

   ....

   ....

   ....

   ....

   ....
   (6 marks)

2   Study **Figure 2**, which is a diagram of a chalk and clay landscape.

   Figure 2

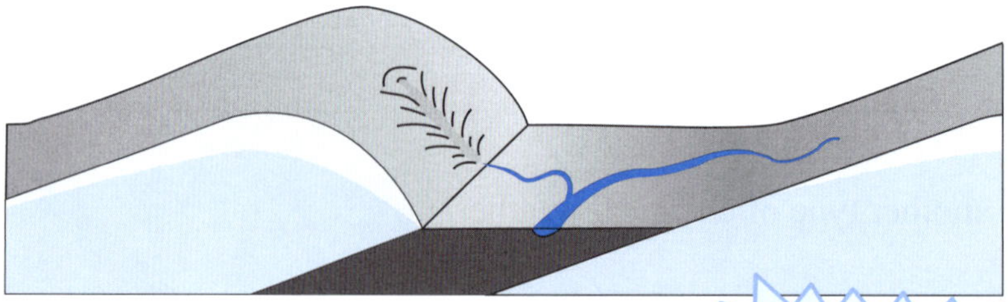

   (a) Label **Figure 2** to show the characteristics of the landscape.

   Keep labels clear and make sure you mark each feature with its own label.
   (4 marks)

   (b) Explain why spring lines form in a chalk and clay landscape.

   ....

   ....

   ....
   (3 marks)

Unit 1A — Rocks, Resources and Scenery

Rocks and Landscapes

3   Study **Figure 3**, which shows a gorge in a Carboniferous limestone landscape.

Figure 3

(a) Explain how the gorge in **Figure 3** may have been formed.

Make sure you refer to the gorge in the photo.

....

....

....

....

....

....

(4 marks)

(b) (i) Describe the formation of stalactites and stalagmites.

....

....

(2 marks)

   (ii) Name the underground feature formed when a stalactite and a stalagmite join together.

....

(1 mark)

(c) **Figure 4** is a diagram of a limestone landscape.
Label **Figure 4** to show the features of the landscape.

(4 marks)

Figure 4

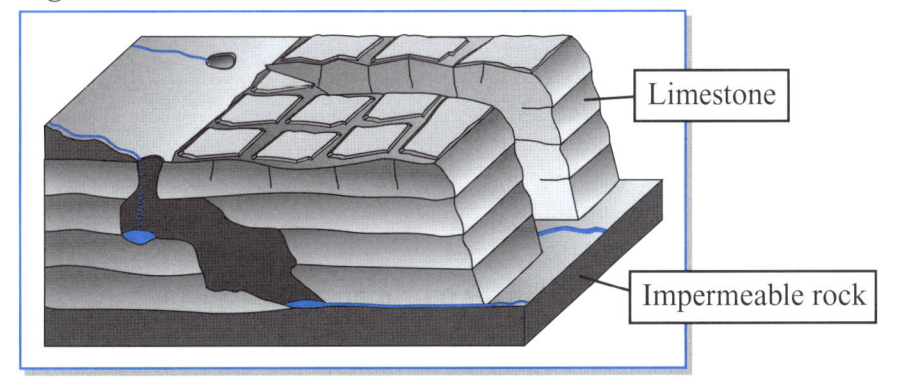

— Limestone

— Impermeable rock

(d) (i) What are resurgent rivers?

....

(1 mark)

   (ii) Give one fact about limestone that results in the formation of dry valleys.

....

(1 mark)

Unit 1A — Rocks, Resources and Scenery

Using Landscapes

1   **Figure 1** is a table of data which shows the number of different farms in a granite landscape in the UK in 1990 and 2005. **Figure 2** is a graph made from the data in **Figure 1**.

Figure 1

Farm type	1990	2005
	Number of holdings	
Livestock (cattle and sheep)	820	650
Dairy	250	110
Cereals	40	60
TOTAL	1110	820

Figure 2

(a) (i) Use **Figure 1** to complete **Figure 2**.
(2 marks)

Make sure the top of your bar is at the total number of holdings — if it's not, check for mistakes.

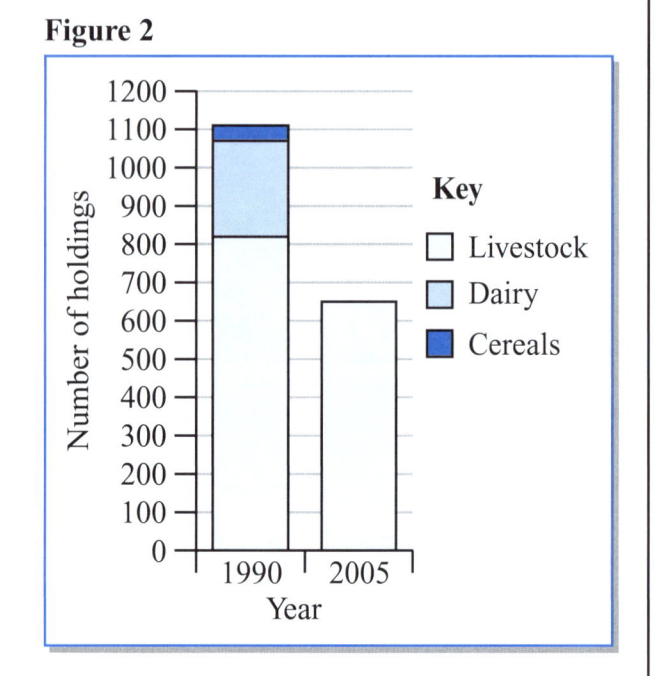

(ii) Using **Figures 1** and **2**, describe and explain the pattern of farming in this area in 1990.

....

....

....

....
(4 marks)

(b) Describe other ways that granite landscapes can be used.

....

....

....
(3 marks)

(c) Why are chalk landscapes useful for providing a water supply?

....

....
(2 marks)

2   For **either** a chalk and clay **or** a granite landscape that you have studied, describe how the area has been used for farming and other activities. Circle the one you choose to write about.

Chalk and clay   **Granite**

(8 marks)

Unit 1A — Rocks, Resources and Scenery

Using Landscapes

3   Study **Figure 3**, which shows the number of tourists that visited different national parks in Boulderland in 2008.

(a) (i) Using **Figure 3**, calculate the number of tourists that visited the limestone landscape.

....

....

....

....
(2 marks)

Figure 3

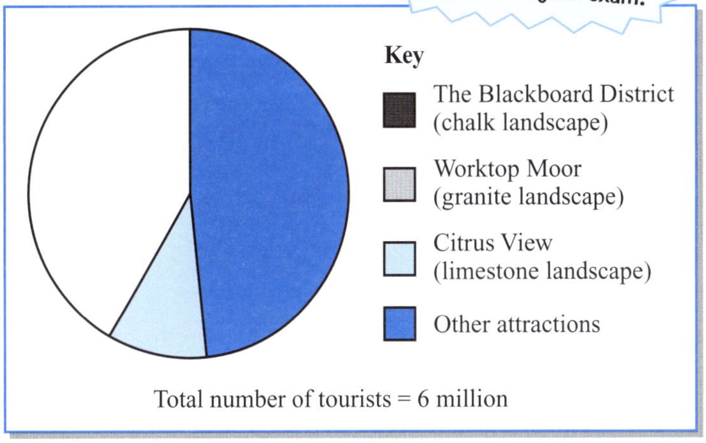

Key
- ■ The Blackboard District (chalk landscape)
- ▨ Worktop Moor (granite landscape)
- ▢ Citrus View (limestone landscape)
- ■ Other attractions

Total number of tourists = 6 million

Make sure you know how to use a protractor before you go into your exam.

(ii) In 2008, 1 million tourists visited Worktop Moor and 1.5 million tourists visited The Blackboard District. Complete **Figure 3** to show this, and show your working.

....
(2 marks)

(b) Give two uses of quarried limestone.

....

....
(2 marks)

(c) Describe why limestone landscapes are popular tourist attractions.

....

....
(2 marks)

(d) Describe the costs and benefits of tourism in scenic landscapes.

....

....

....

....

Remember — 'describe' means you just have to say what things are like, you don't have to say why they're like that.

....

....
(6 marks)

4   Using named examples, describe how different rock landscapes are quarried for resources and used for tourism.

(8 marks)

Unit 1A — Rocks, Resources and Scenery

Quarrying Impacts

1 Study **Figure 1** and **Figure 2**, which show the front page of a newspaper and an aerial plan of a proposed limestone quarry near the town of Himilton.

Figure 1

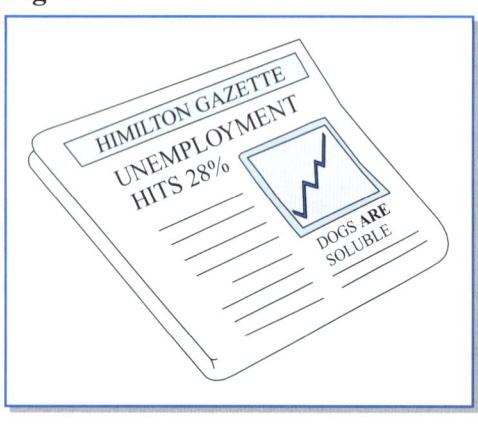

HIMILTON GAZETTE
UNEMPLOYMENT HITS 28%
DOGS ARE SOLUBLE

Figure 2

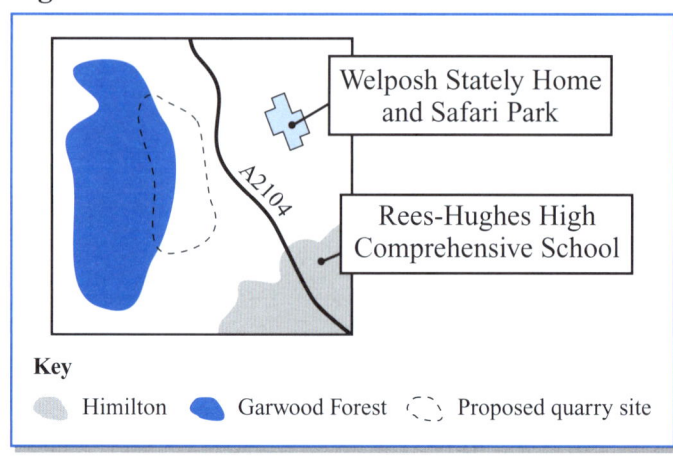

- Welposh Stately Home and Safari Park
- Rees-Hughes High Comprehensive School
- A2104

Key: Himilton | Garwood Forest | Proposed quarry site

(a) Using **Figure 1** and **Figure 2**, give advantages and disadvantages of the proposed quarry.

....

....

....

....

It can help to categorise advantages and disadvantages as social, economic or environmental.

....

....

(6 marks)

(b) Study **Figure 3**, which shows the estimated volume of limestone that will be extracted from the quarry each year.

The proposed site contains 400 000 m³ of limestone. How much limestone would be left at the site by the end of year 3 if the quarry was in use?

....
(1 mark)

Figure 3

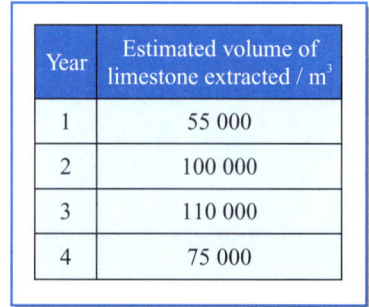

Year	Estimated volume of limestone extracted / m³
1	55 000
2	100 000
3	110 000
4	75 000

(c) Suggest a use for the quarry site after it has been closed down.

....
(1 mark)

2 Describe the economic, social and environmental advantages and disadvantages of a quarry that you have studied.

(8 marks)

Unit 1A — Rocks, Resources and Scenery

Quarrying Management

1   Study **Figure 1**, which shows extracts from three articles about Tunstead Quarry, Derbyshire.

(a) (i) Explain what sustainable management is.

Figure 1

> Trials have shown that chips of old rubber tyres can be used to replace around 50% of the fossil fuels used to run the cement kiln at Tunstead.

> **NEW RAIL SERVICE TO REPLACE 24 000 LORRY TRIPS**
> Funding secures new facilities

> In 2004, a new cement processing plant was opened at Tunstead Quarry. The plant is 40% more energy efficient and it produces 60% fewer sulfur dioxides and 9% fewer nitrogen oxides.

....
....
....
....
....
....
....
(3 marks)

(ii) Using **Figure 1**, describe and explain how the new cement processing plant has improved the sustainability of Tunstead Quarry.

There are three articles in Figure 1 — you might not have to use all three for every question on Figure 1.

....
....
....
....
(4 marks)

(iii) Explain how the fuel trials and new rail facilities could affect the quarry's sustainability.

....
....
(2 marks)

(b) Quarries can also be sustainably managed by restoring natural habitats after the quarry closes.

(i) Explain why this is a sustainable management strategy.

....
(1 mark)

(ii) Suggest ways that the restored parts of a quarry could be used.

....
....
(2 marks)

2   For a quarry that you have studied, describe the sustainable management strategies that are being used there.

(8 marks)

Unit 1A — Rocks, Resources and Scenery

Unit 1A — Weather and Climate

UK Climate

1   Study **Figures 1** and **2**. **Figure 1** shows climate graphs for two places in the UK. **Figure 2** shows the location of these two places in the UK.

Figure 1

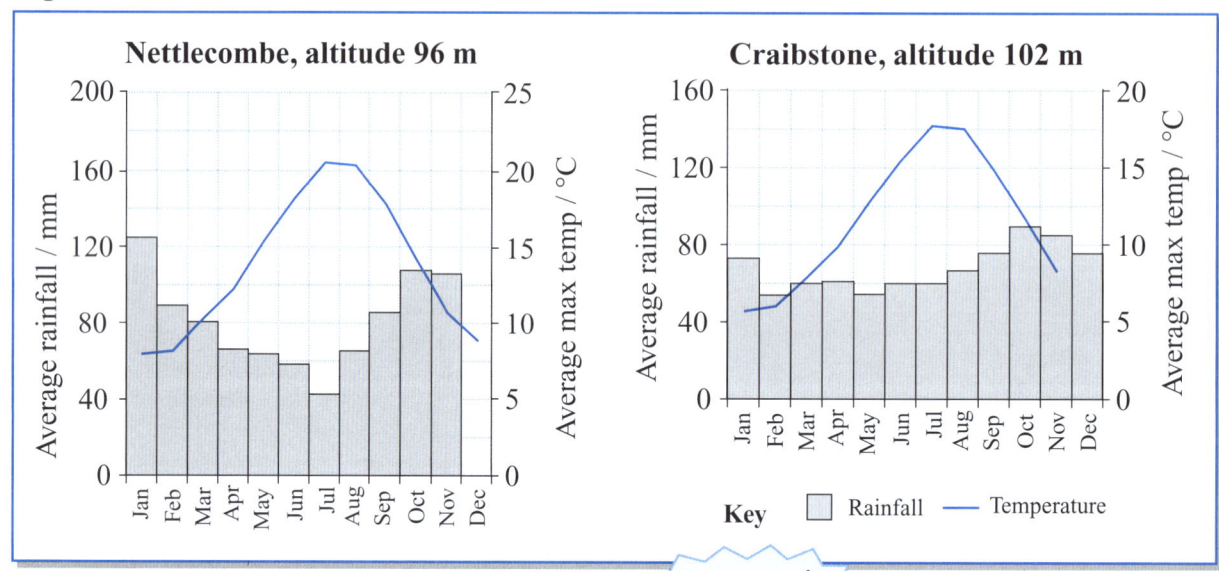

[Climate graphs: Nettlecombe, altitude 96 m; Craibstone, altitude 102 m. Key: Rainfall (bars), Temperature (line).]

Figure 2

[Map of the UK showing Craibstone in northeast Scotland and Nettlecombe in southwest England.]

(a) Complete the graphs in **Figure 1** by adding the following data to them:

Always use a ruler when you're filling in lines and bars on graphs.

   (i)   The average December rainfall in Nettlecombe is 129 mm.
   (1 mark)

   (ii) The average maximum December temperature in Craibstone is 6.4 °C.
   (1 mark)

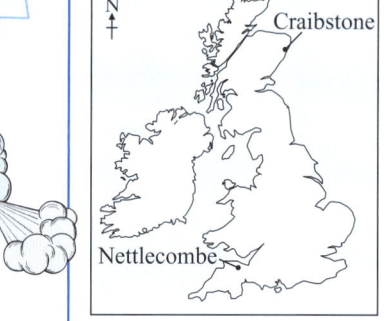

(b) Using **Figure 1**, describe the differences in climate between Nettlecombe and Craibstone.

You just need to talk about rainfall and temperature — that's all the figure shows.

....
....
....
....
(4 marks)

(c) (i) Explain the difference in temperature between Nettlecombe and Craibstone.

....
....
....
....
(4 marks)

Unit 1A — Weather and Climate

UK Climate

(ii) Explain the difference in average monthly rainfall between Nettlecombe and Craibstone.

....

....

....

....

....
(4 marks)

Figure 3

2   Study **Figure 3**, which shows climate graphs for the whole of the UK.

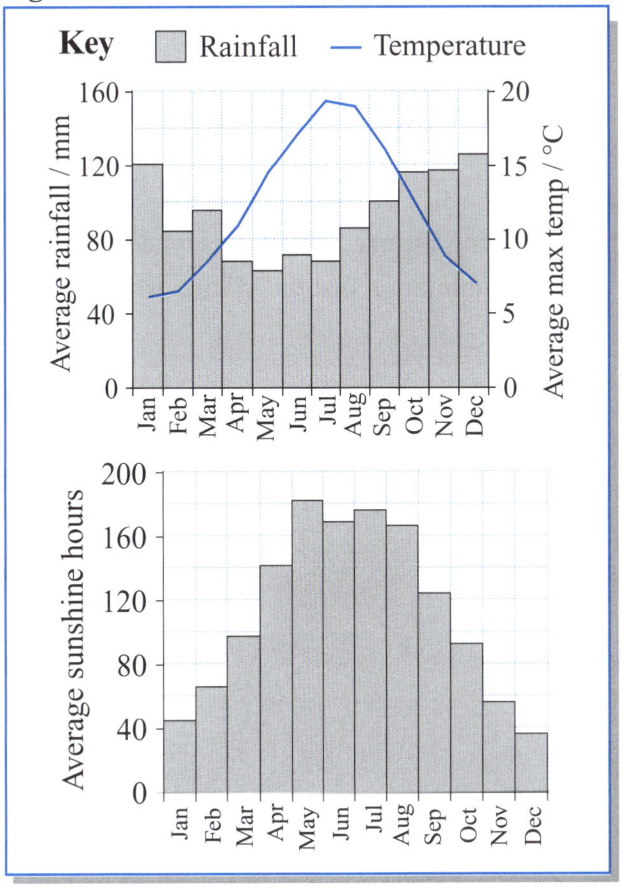

(a) (i) In what month does the UK get the highest amount of rainfall?

....
(1 mark)

(ii) How many sunshine hours are there on average in October in the UK?

....
(1 mark)

(b) Using **Figure 3**, describe the climate of the UK.

....

....

....

....

....

....

....
(6 marks)

> Because it says 'Using Figure 3' you just have to describe the patterns you can see on the graphs.

(c) Give two factors that explain why the UK has a mild climate with wet and dry weather.

....

....
(2 marks)

Unit 1A — Weather and Climate

Depressions and Anticyclones

1 Study **Figure 1**, which shows a depression approaching a village.

(a) (i) Complete the key in **Figure 1**.

(1 mark)

(ii) Describe how a depression forms.

(4 marks)

Figure 1

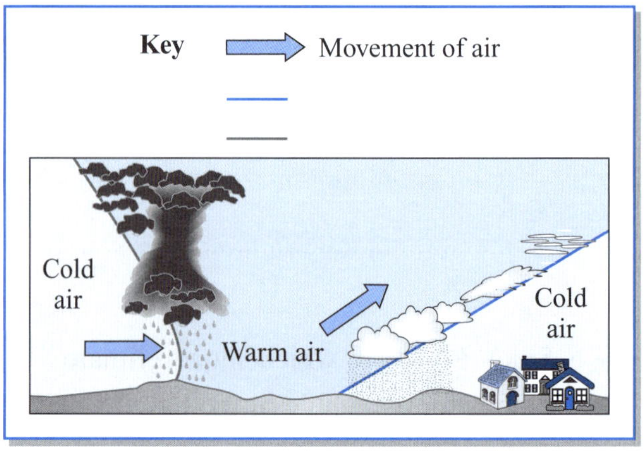
Key
Movement of air
Cold air
Warm air
Cold air

(b) Using **Figure 1** and your own knowledge, describe the changes in temperature and precipitation that the village would experience as the depression passes over it.

You just need to describe the changes in weather here, there's no need to explain them.

(6 marks)

2 Study **Figure 2**, which shows the average air pressure in Derby over a period of six weeks.

Figure 2

Week	1	2	3	4	5	6
Pressure (mbar)	990	998	1008	1004	1036	1006

(a) In which week did an anticyclone pass over Derby?

(1 mark)

(b) Explain the differences in the weather caused by anticyclones in summer and in winter.

(4 marks)

Extreme UK Weather

1   Study **Figure 1**, which is an article about the climate of the UK.

Figure 1

> **UK feels the heat of climate change**
> Average temperature in the UK is increasing. Between 1995 and 2004, the UK had six of the ten warmest years since 1861. The hottest temperature ever recorded in the UK was in 2003 — it reached 38.5 °C in Kent. Rainfall is also increasing — the summer of 2007 was the wettest on record and rainfall is also becoming more intense.

(a) (i) Use **Figure 1** to describe the evidence that UK temperature is becoming more extreme.

....

....

....

(2 marks)

(ii) Suggest two extreme weather events that the changes described in **Figure 1** could cause.

....

(2 marks)

(b) (i) Describe the negative impacts of extreme weather on transport and agriculture.

....

....

....

(3 marks)

(ii) Describe how the negative impacts of extreme weather can be reduced.

....

....

....

....

....

....

(6 marks)

(c) Suggest how more extreme weather in the UK could have positive impacts on agriculture and people's health.

> The number of marks is a clue for how much to write — there are three marks so you only need to write about three impacts.

....

....

....

....

(3 marks)

Unit 1A — Weather and Climate

Global Climate Change — Debate

1. Study **Figure 1**, which shows global temperature between 1860 and 2000.

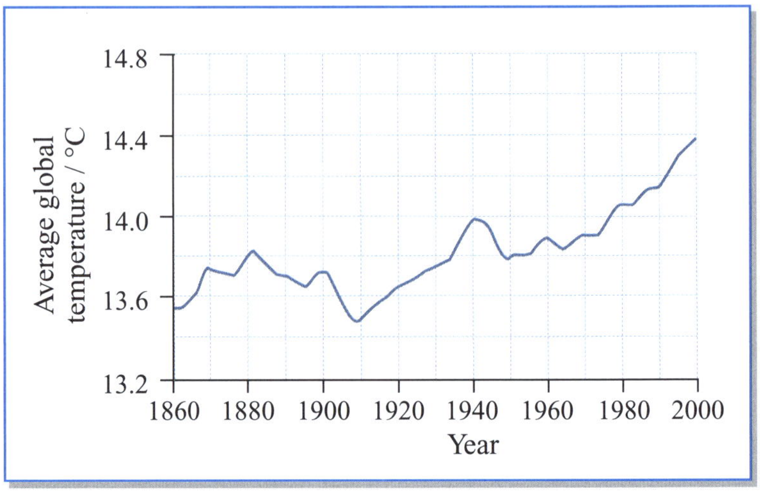

    (a) What is climate change?

    ....

    ....

    ....

    ....
    (1 mark)

    Figure 1

    [Graph showing Average global temperature / °C (y-axis, 13.2 to 14.8) against Year (x-axis, 1860 to 2000)]

    (b) (i) How much did global temperature rise by between 1860 and 2000?

    ....
    (1 mark)

    (ii) Describe the change in average global temperature shown by the graph.

    ....

    ....
    (2 marks)

    (c) Describe one other source of evidence that shows an increase in global temperature.

    ....
    (1 mark)

    (d) There is a scientific consensus that global warming is caused by human activity.

    (i) Explain how human activity has caused global warming.

    This question is level marked so think about your sentence structure, grammar and punctuation.

    ....

    ....

    ....

    ....

    ....
    (6 marks)

    (ii) Describe and explain another factor that can cause the Earth's climate to change.

    ....

    ....
    (2 marks)

Unit 1A — Weather and Climate

Global Climate Change — Impacts

1   Study **Figure 1**, which shows data on sea level rise between 1900 and 2100.

Figure 1

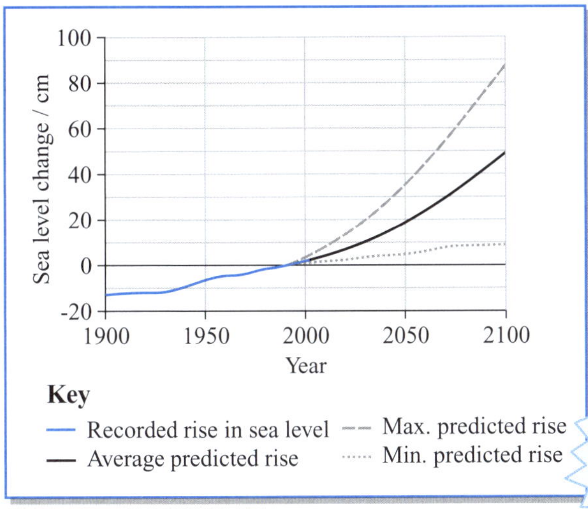

(a) Sea level rise is caused by global warming. State one global impact of sea level rise.

....

....

(1 mark)

(b) What is the average predicted rise in sea level between 2050 and 2100?

....

Remember to include the units when giving readings from a graph.

(1 mark)

(c) Give two other global environmental impacts of global warming.

....

....

(2 marks)

2   Study **Figure 2**, which shows the maize yield for a low latitude farm in Central Africa.

Figure 2

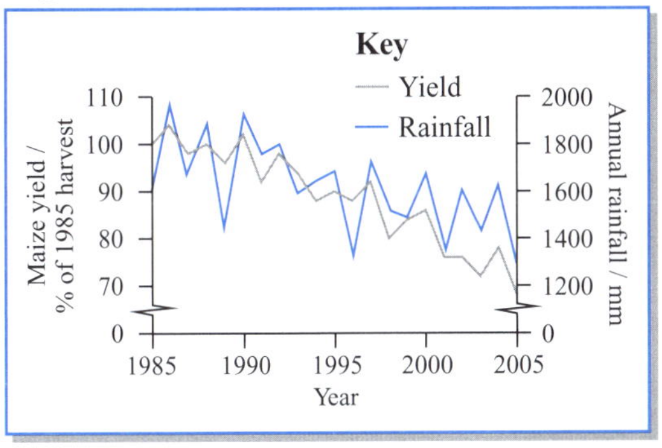

(a) (i) Using **Figure 2**, describe how climate change may be affecting crop yields in low latitude areas.

....

....

....

(2 marks)

(ii) Suggest one economic and one social impact of the trends shown in **Figure 2**.

....

....

(2 marks)

(b) What are the potential impacts of climate change in the UK?

....

Make sure the impacts you write about are specific to the UK.

....

....

....

(4 marks)

Unit 1A — Weather and Climate

Global Climate Change — Responses

1 The Kyoto Protocol is an international response to climate change.

(a) (i) What have countries that have signed the Kyoto Protocol agreed to do?

....

....
(2 marks)

(ii) Explain how the carbon credits trading scheme works.

....

....

....
(3 marks)

(iii) Describe one factor that might limit the effectiveness of the Kyoto Protocol as a response to climate change.

....
(1 mark)

(b) Study **Figure 1**, which shows the price of car tax for cars with different CO_2 emissions. Explain how **Figure 1** shows a national response to reduce the threat of global climate change.

Figure 1

CO_2 emissions (g/km)	12 months tax (£)
111-120	35.00
121-130	120.00
131-140	120.00
141-150	125.00
151-165	150.00
166-175	175.00
176-185	175.00
186-200	215.00
201-225	215.00
226-255	405.00

....

....

....
(2 marks)

(c) Responses to the threat of climate change need to be international, national and local. Suggest some local responses and explain how they reduce the threat of climate change.

> Start your answer by stating the response and describing what it is — don't just dive straight into explaining it.

....

....

....

....

....

....
(6 marks)

Unit 1A — Weather and Climate

Tropical Storms

1 Study **Figure 1**, which shows a cross section of a tropical storm.

(a) (i) Label **Figure 1** to show the characteristics of a tropical storm.

(4 marks)

Figure 1

Add at least as many labels as there are marks.

(ii) Give two other characteristics of tropical storms.

....

....

....

....

(2 marks)

(b) Using **Figure 2**, describe and explain the global distribution of tropical storms.

Figure 2

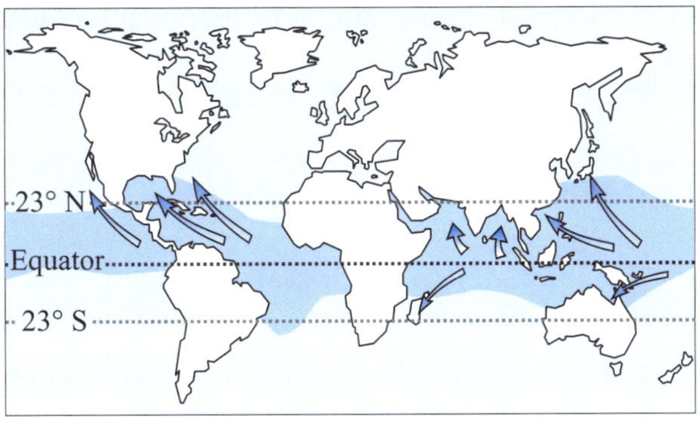

Key
- path of tropical storm
- sea surface temperature 27 °C or higher

....

....

....

....

....

....

....

....

....

(6 marks)

(c) Why do tropical storms lose strength when they move over land?

....

(1 mark)

2 Using case studies of tropical storms in rich and poor parts of the world, compare the short and long-term responses.

(8 marks)

Unit 1A — Weather and Climate

Ecosystems

1   Study **Figure 1**, which shows a coastal food chain.

Figure 1

Seaweed → Periwinkle → Crab → Octopus

(a) (i)   Which of the organisms in the food chain shown in **Figure 1** is the producer?

....
(1 mark)

(ii)   What is meant by the term 'consumer'?

....
(1 mark)

(iii)   Give an example of a consumer from the food chain shown in **Figure 1**.

....
(1 mark)

(b) What does a food web show?

....
(1 mark)

(c) Explain how the organisms in the food chain shown in **Figure 1** might be affected if a disease reduced the crab population.

....

....

> Think about how the population of each organism in the food chain might change.

....
(3 marks)

(d) Describe how nutrients are cycled in ecosystems.

....

....

....

....
(4 marks)

World Ecosystems

1   Study **Figure 1**, which shows the global distribution of tropical rainforests.

    Figure 1

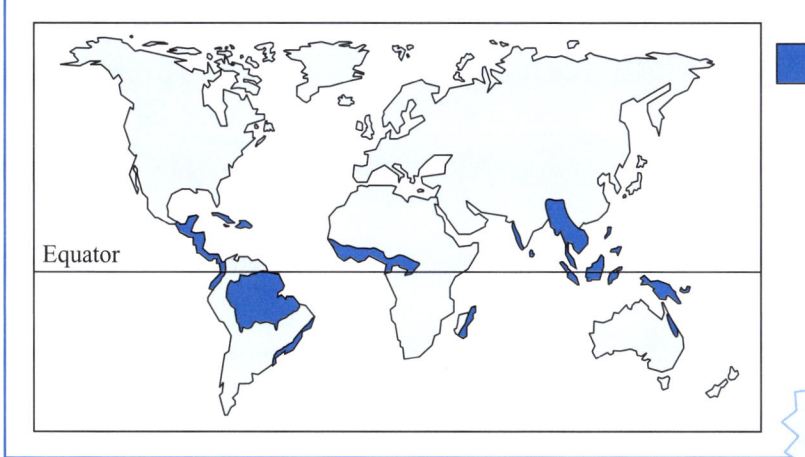

    Use Figure 1 to help you name some areas where they're found.

    (a) (i)   Describe the global distribution of tropical rainforests.

        ....

        ....
        (2 marks)

    (ii) Explain why tropical rainforests are found in these areas.

        ....

        ....
        (2 marks)

    (b) Describe the characteristics of the soil and vegetation in a tropical rainforest.

        ....

        ....

        ....

        ....

        ....

        ....
        (6 marks)

    (c) Explain two ways in which rainforest plants are adapted to their environment.

        There are four marks available here so make sure you describe two ways and explain them both.

        ....

        ....

        ....

        ....
        (4 marks)

Unit 1A — The Living World

World Ecosystems

2 Study **Figure 2**, which shows a diagram of a desert cactus.

Figure 2
(Thick skin, Spines, Long roots)

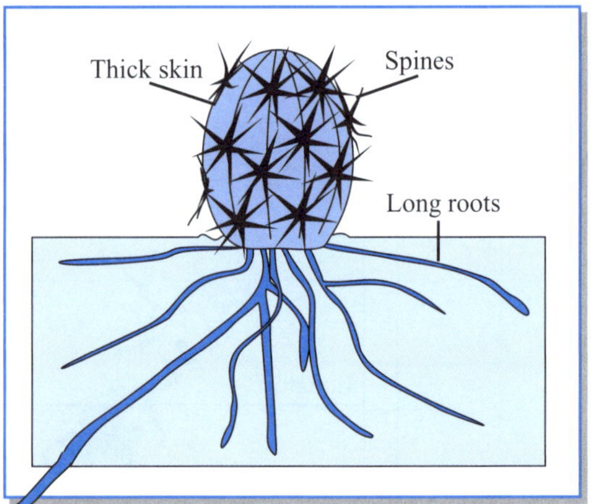

(a) Use **Figure 2** to explain how plants are adapted to a hot desert climate.

....

....

....

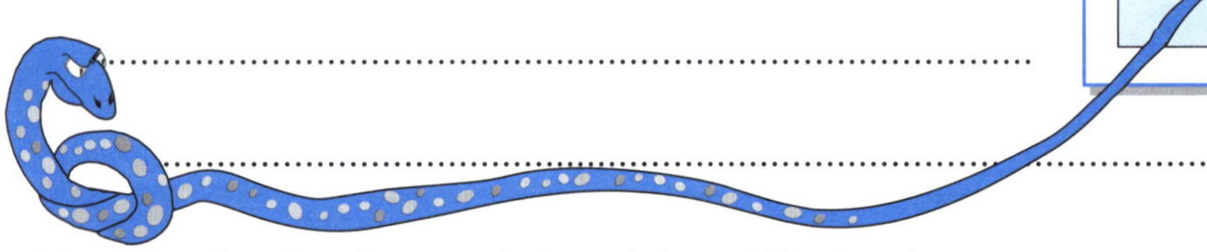

....
(3 marks)

(b) Describe the characteristics of the soil in hot deserts.

....

....
(2 marks)

3 Study **Figure 3**, which shows climate data for a hot desert.

Figure 3

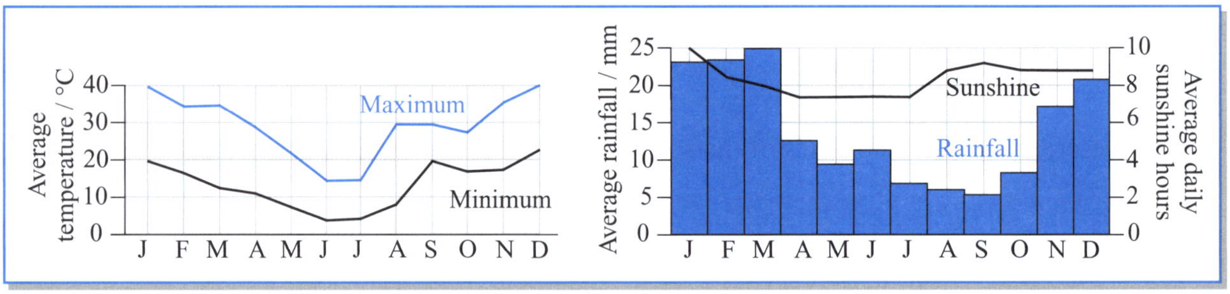

(a) (i) Which month has the highest average rainfall?

....
(1 mark)

(ii) What is the average maximum temperature for December?   *Don't forget the units.*

....
(1 mark)

(b) With reference to **Figure 3**, describe the characteristics of the hot desert climate.

....

....

....

....
(4 marks)

Unit 1A — The Living World

World Ecosystems

4   Study **Figure 4**, which shows temperature and rainfall data for an area of temperate deciduous forest.

Figure 4

Month	Average temperature / °C	Average rainfall / mm
January	2	64
February	5	42
March	6	33
April	12	42
May	19	45
June	19	48
July	21	69
August	19	62
September	12	45
October	10	55
November	4	65
December	2	52

(a) (i) Which month has the highest average temperature?

....
(1 mark)

(ii) Use **Figure 4** to describe the climate of this temperate deciduous forest.

....

....

....

....

....
(2 marks)

(b) Describe the global distribution of temperate deciduous forests.

....

....

....
(2 marks)

(c) Describe the vegetation found in a temperate deciduous forest.

The question asks about vegetation in general so you can include the vegetation structure and plant adaptations.

....

....

....

....

....

....
(6 marks)

(d) Explain what the soil is like in a temperate deciduous forest.

....

....
(2 marks)

Unit 1A — The Living World

Temperate Deciduous Forest

1   Study **Figure 1**, a bar chart showing how visitors use a temperate deciduous forest.

    Figure 1

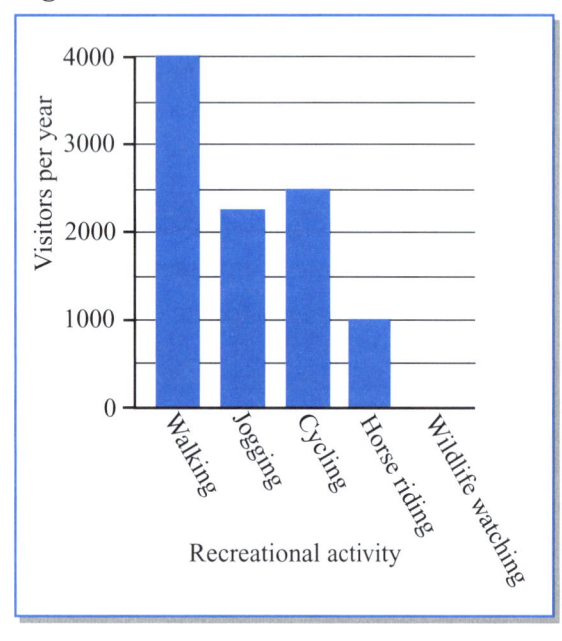

    (a) (i)   How many visitors use the forest for jogging each year?

              ....
              (1 mark)

        (ii) Complete the bar chart to show that 2750 visitors use the forest for wildlife watching each year.
              (1 mark)

        (iii) How many people in total use the forest each year?

              ....
              ....
              (1 mark)

        (iv) What percentage of visitors use the forest for horse riding?

              ....
              (1 mark)

    (b) Suggest two other uses of temperate deciduous forests that aren't shown in **Figure 1**.

        ....
        ....
        (2 marks)

    (c) Suggest how the activities in **Figure 1** could have a negative impact on the forest.

        ....
        ....
        ....
        ....
        ....
        ....
        (6 marks)

2   Explain whether the strategies used to manage a temperate deciduous forest you have studied are sustainable.

    (8 marks)

Unit 1A — The Living World

Tropical Rainforest — Deforestation

1 Study **Figure 1**, a series of maps showing the extent of deforestation in an area of tropical rainforest between 1958 and 2008.

Figure 1

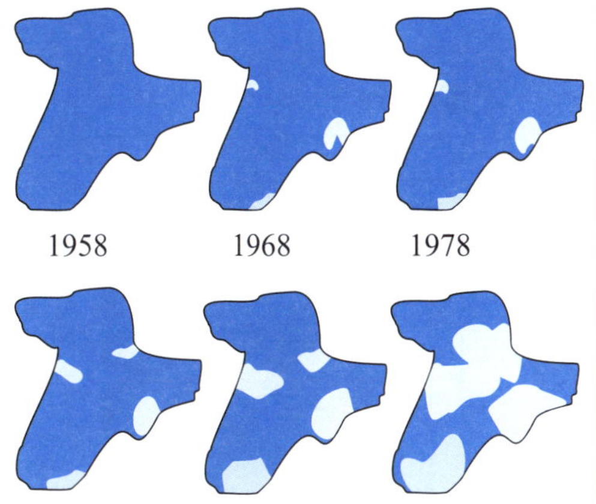

1958   1968   1978

1988   1998   2008

Key ■ Forested   □ Deforested

(a) With reference to **Figure 1**, describe the changes to the rainforest between 1958 and 2008.

....
....
....
....
....
(4 marks)

(b) Explain three possible causes of deforestation in this area.

In level marked questions, you need to structure your answer so it flows well.

....
....
....
....
....
....
(6 marks)

(c) Give two advantages of deforestation.

....
....
(2 marks)

(d) Describe and explain the environmental impacts of rainforest deforestation.

....
....
....
....
....

Always re-read long answers to check your answer makes sense and it's all spelt correctly.

....
(6 marks)

Unit 1A — The Living World

Tropical Rainforest — Sustainable Management

1   Study **Figure 1**, part of a newspaper article on the Amazon Education Project in Brazil.

Figure 1

Education Scheme Offers Hope for Amazon Rainforest

Brazilian environmentalists have set up an Education Project that aims to educate the local population about the devastating impacts of deforestation.

The project manager Silverado Arboles said: "The local population is reliant on the rainforest, but the problem is that they can make a lot of money from illegal logging.

Hardwoods such as mahogany fetch high prices so it is hard to find alternative sources of income that pay as much".

The project also aims to help locals to sustainably manage the forest — it runs schemes to teach locals selective logging techniques, and it provides discounted tree saplings for replanting schemes.

(a) What is meant by 'the sustainable management of tropical rainforests'?

....

....
(2 marks)

(b) Use evidence from **Figure 1** to describe how forests can be sustainably managed.

....

....

....

....
(4 marks)

(c) How might increasing taxes on importing mahogany reduce deforestation?

....

....

....
(3 marks)

(d) Suggest how the education part of the project discussed in **Figure 1** helps towards the sustainable management of a tropical rainforest.

....

Felling = bad
Hugging = good

....

....

....
(4 marks)

Unit 1A — The Living World

Tropical Rainforest — Sustainable Management

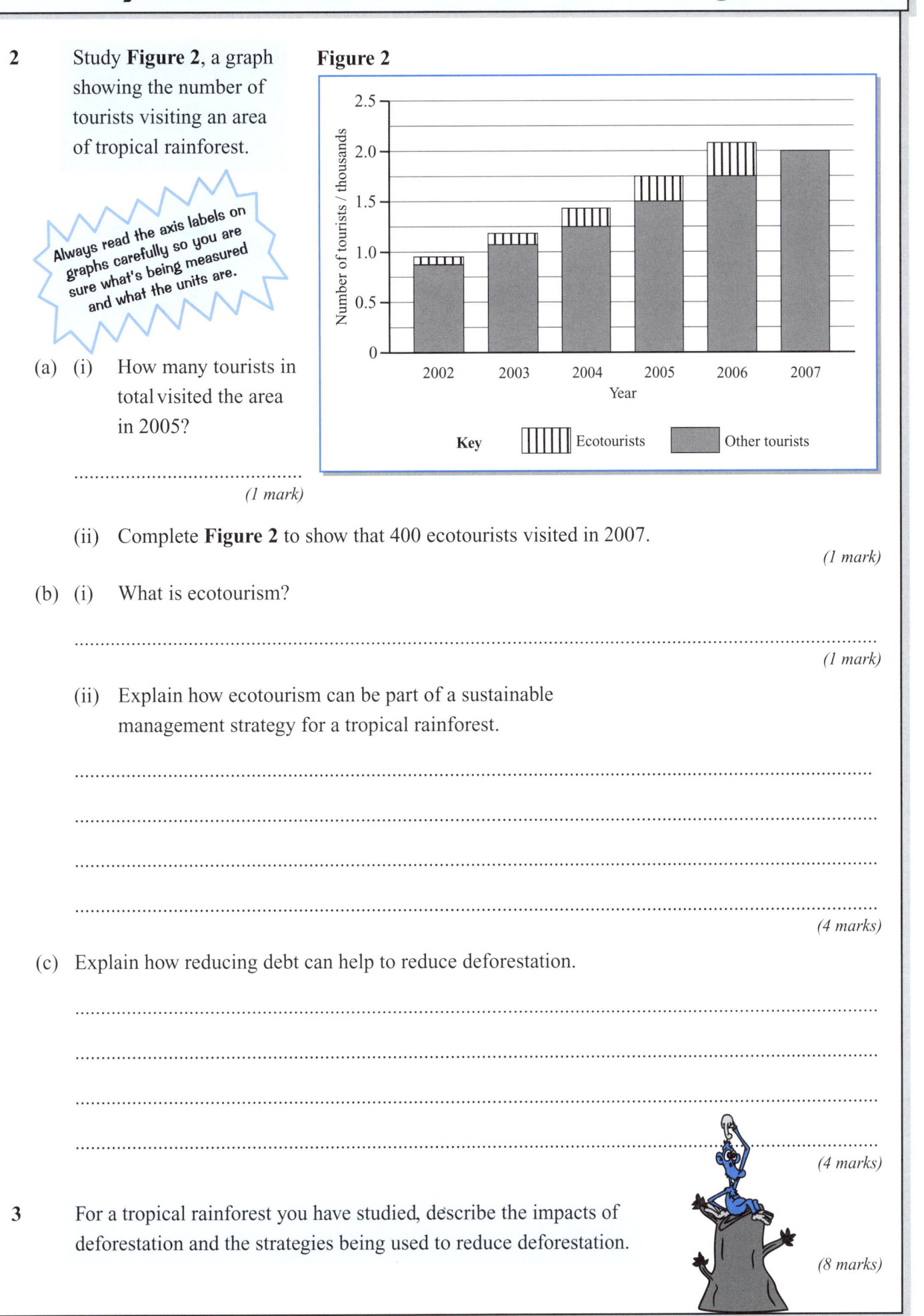

2   Study **Figure 2**, a graph showing the number of tourists visiting an area of tropical rainforest.

Figure 2

Always read the axis labels on graphs carefully so you are sure what's being measured and what the units are.

(a) (i) How many tourists in total visited the area in 2005?

....
(1 mark)

(ii) Complete **Figure 2** to show that 400 ecotourists visited in 2007.
(1 mark)

(b) (i) What is ecotourism?

....
(1 mark)

(ii) Explain how ecotourism can be part of a sustainable management strategy for a tropical rainforest.

....

....

....

....
(4 marks)

(c) Explain how reducing debt can help to reduce deforestation.

....

....

....

....
(4 marks)

3   For a tropical rainforest you have studied, describe the impacts of deforestation and the strategies being used to reduce deforestation.

(8 marks)

Unit 1A — The Living World

Hot Deserts

1 Study **Figure 1**, which shows the global distribution of hot deserts and some of their main uses.

Figure 1

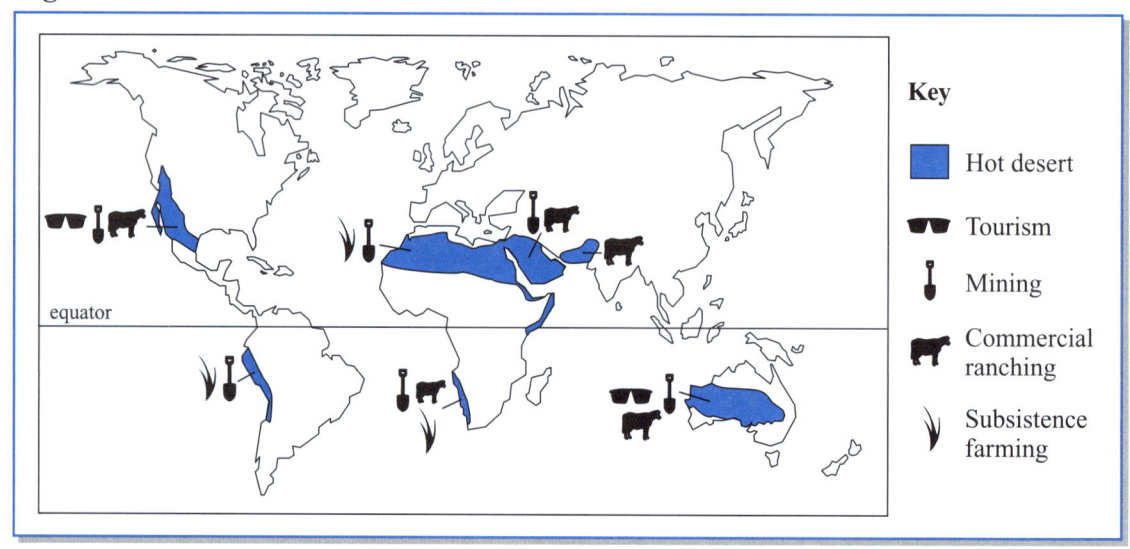

Key:
- Hot desert
- Tourism
- Mining
- Commercial ranching
- Subsistence farming

(a) Use evidence from **Figure 1** to describe and compare the main uses of hot deserts in rich and poor countries.

When answering questions like this try to use names of countries and regions in your answer.

....

....

....

....

....

....
(6 marks)

(b) Suggest why some deserts may be experiencing an increase in population. Give reasons for your answer.

....

....
(2 marks)

(c) Describe two negative impacts of the uses of hot deserts.

....

....
(2 marks)

2 For a named hot desert, describe how management strategies are used to ensure sustainable use of the area.

(8 marks)

Unit 1A — The Living World

The River Valley

1   Study **Figure 1**, which shows the long profile of a river.

(a) Complete **Figure 1** by labelling the source and mouth of the river.

(1 mark)

Figure 1

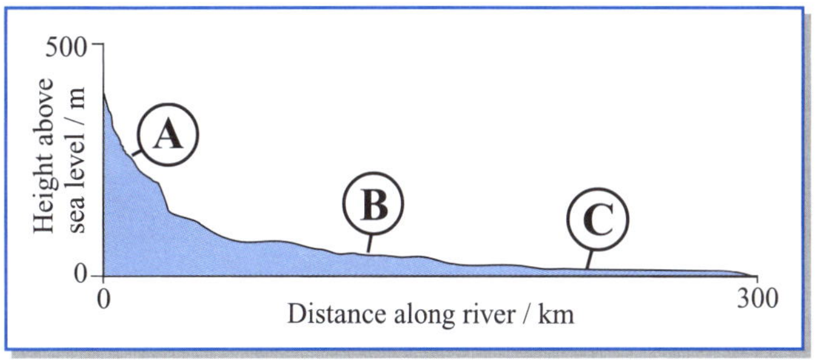

(b) (i) What is the difference between the long profile and the cross profile of a river?

....

....

....

(2 marks)

(ii) Describe the cross profile at the points labelled A and B in **Figure 1**.

Cross profile at point A ....

....

Cross profile at point B ....

....

(4 marks)

(iii) Draw a labelled sketch showing the cross profile that you would expect at the point labelled C in **Figure 1**.

Use a pencil to draw diagrams, then you can rub out any mistakes.

(3 marks)

(c) Explain why the upper course of a river valley has a different cross profile from the lower course.

....

....

....

....

(4 marks)

Erosion, Transportation and Deposition

1   Study **Figure 1**, which shows how the velocity of the River Dance varies along its course.

(a) (i) Small gravel particles are transported by velocities above 0.1 m per second. At what distance along the River Dance does the transportation of gravel start?

....
(1 mark)

Figure 1

(ii) At 80 km along the River Dance, pebbles are being transported. Give the velocity of the river at this point and name the process by which pebbles are transported.

....
....
....

Use a ruler to read off a graph accurately.

(2 marks)

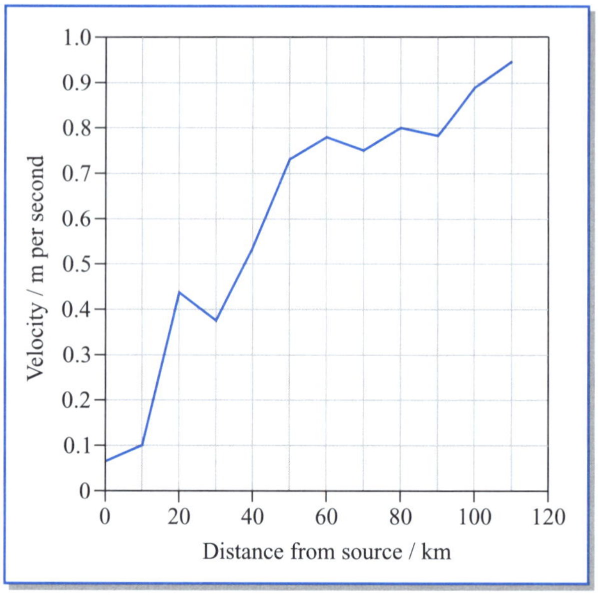

(iii) Name and describe two other processes by which material is transported in rivers.

....
....
....
....
(4 marks)

(b) Describe the four processes of erosion taking place in the River Dance.

....
....
....
....
(4 marks)

(c) Deposition occurs when rivers slow down. Describe four reasons why rivers slow down.

....
....
....
....
(4 marks)

Unit 1B — Water on the Land

River Landforms

1 Study **Figure 1**, which is a labelled photograph of a meander.

(a) (i) Suggest a feature likely to be found at the part of the river labelled A in **Figure 1** and explain its formation.

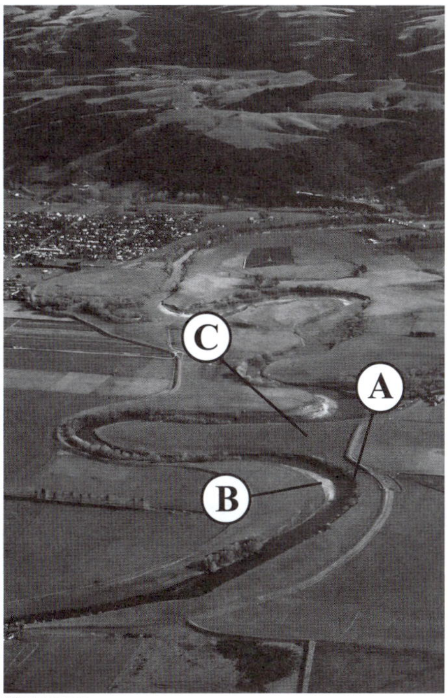

Figure 1

....

....

....

....

....

Look closely at the labels to make sure you're writing about the correct feature.

....

(3 marks)

(ii) Suggest a feature likely to be found at the part of the river labelled B in **Figure 1** and explain its formation.

....

....

....

(3 marks)

(b) (i) Name the feature labelled C in **Figure 1**.

....

(1 mark)

(ii) Explain how an ox-bow lake could form on the river shown in **Figure 1**.

....

This is a six mark question so make sure you include lots of detail and specific geographical terms.

....

....

....

....

....

(6 marks)

Unit 1B — Water on the Land

River Landforms

2 Study **Figure 2**, which is an Ordnance Survey® map showing part of Snowdonia, Wales.

Figure 2

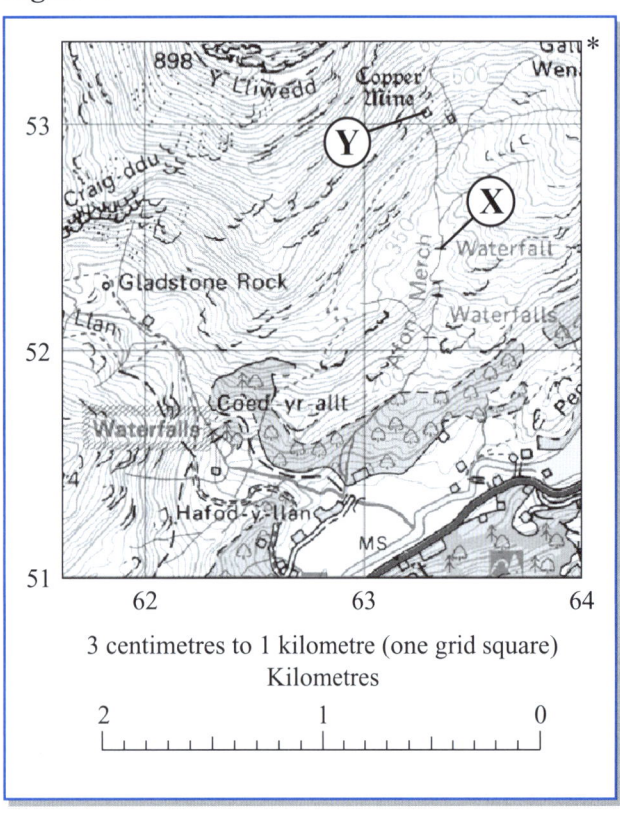

3 centimetres to 1 kilometre (one grid square)
Kilometres

(a) Use evidence from **Figure 2** to show that the Afon Merch is an upper course stream.

....
....
....
....
....
....
....
....

Study the map carefully — you need to find at least four pieces of evidence.

(4 marks)

(b) (i) A waterfall is found at point X on **Figure 2**. Give the six figure grid reference for the waterfall.

....
(1 mark)

(ii) A copper mine is found at point Y on **Figure 2**. State the distance in kilometres between the mine and the waterfall.

....
(1 mark)

(c) (i) Describe how waterfalls are formed.

....
....
....
....
....
(4 marks)

(ii) Name the landform that is left as a waterfall retreats.

....
(1 mark)

Unit 1B — Water on the Land

River Landforms

3   Study **Figure 3**, which shows a photograph of a river valley.

(a) (i) Label **Figure 3** to show the flood plain of the river.
(1 mark)

Figure 3

(ii) What is a flood plain?

....
....
....
(1 mark)

(iii) Explain how flood plains are built up.

....
....
....
(3 marks)

(b) (i) What are levees?

....
(1 mark)

(ii) Explain how levees are formed.

....
....
....
(2 marks)

(iii) **Figure 4** is a cross profile diagram of point A shown on **Figure 3**. Draw a labelled sketch showing the levees that could form at this point.

Figure 4

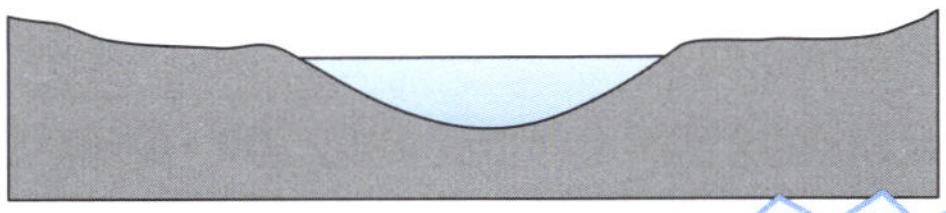

Your sketch doesn't need to be a beautiful drawing — the main thing is to show the levees clearly.

(2 marks)

Unit 1B — Water on the Land

River Discharge

1   Study **Figure 1**, which shows storm hydrographs for two rivers.

Figure 1

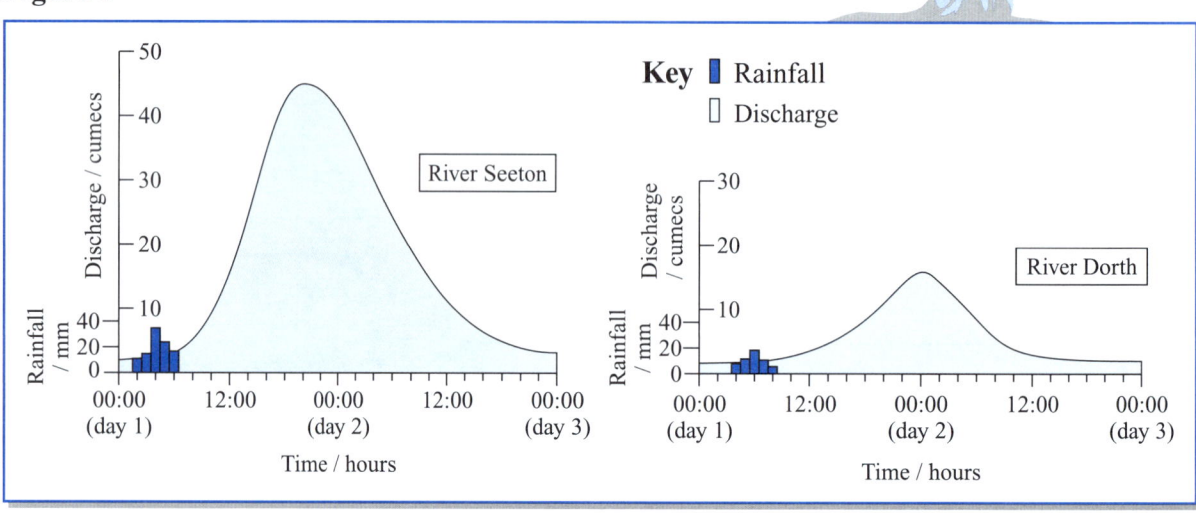

Key: Rainfall / Discharge

River Seeton

River Dorth

(a) (i) Explain what the following terms mean:

Peak discharge ....

Lag time ....
(2 marks)

(ii) At what time was the River Seeton at peak discharge? ....
(1 mark)

(iii) Peak rainfall around the River Dorth was at 06:00 on day 1. What was the lag time?

....
(1 mark)

(b) (i) Contrast the two storm hydrographs shown in **Figure 1**.

....

....

....
(2 marks)

(ii) Suggest reasons why the storm hydrographs are different shapes.

Use info from the Figures as well as your own knowledge to answer questions like this.

....

....

....

....

....
(6 marks)

Unit 1B — Water on the Land

Flooding

1 Study **Figure 1** and **Figure 2**, which show the frequency of flooding of the River Turb and a recent article from a local newspaper.

Figure 1

Year	1997–1998	1998–1999	1999–2000	2000–2001	2001–2002	2002–2003	2003–2004	2004–2005	2005–2006	2006–2007	2007–2008
Number of floods	0	1	1	0	0	2	2	3	2	4	3

Figure 2

RAIN, RAIN, GO AWAY...

Downpours to continue

For the second week in a row there's only one thing in the weather forecast — rain, and lots of it. Despite promises of sunshine, heavy rainfall is expected to hit most places around the county again. Many people are worried that the River Turb, which runs through Sopping, will flood for the second time this year. Scientists have warned that higher than normal snowmelt could make these fears come true.

(a) (i) Describe the trend shown in **Figure 1**.

....
....
....
....
....

There are only two marks available here so your answer should be brief.

(2 marks)

(ii) Using **Figure 2**, explain two physical factors that may cause the River Turb to flood.

....
....
....
....

(4 marks)

(iii) State one other physical factor that would make the River Turb likely to flood.

....

(1 mark)

(b) Describe and explain the human factors that can increase the risk of flooding.

....
....
....
....
....

(6 marks)

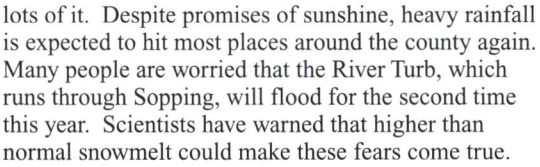

(c) Describe and compare the primary and secondary effects of flooding in rich and poor parts of the world that you have studied.

Only write about the effects — you won't get marks for writing about the responses.

(8 marks)

Unit 1B — Water on the Land

Hard vs Soft Engineering

1 Study **Figure 1**, which shows some of the engineering strategies used to combat flooding along the River Joiner.

Figure 1

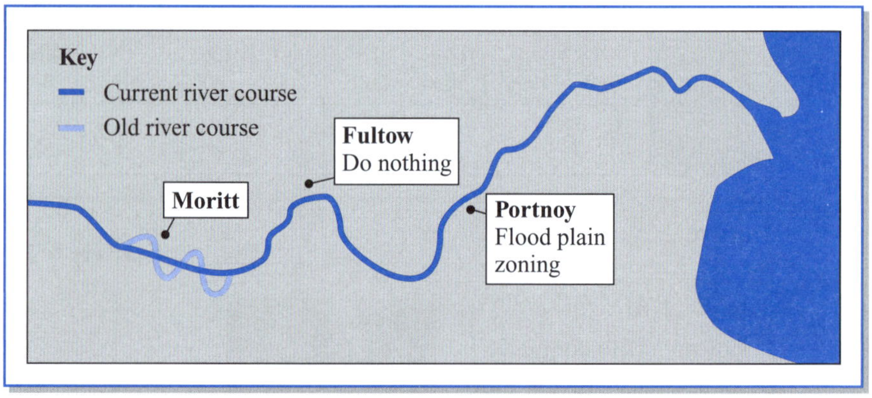

Key
- Current river course
- Old river course

Moritt
Fultow — Do nothing
Portnoy — Flood plain zoning

(a) What is meant by hard and soft engineering strategies?

....
....
....
....
....
....

(2 marks)

(b) (i) What engineering strategy has been used to protect Moritt? Suggest why it could cause problems in Fultow.

....
....

(2 marks)

(ii) Describe the engineering strategy being used at Portnoy and its benefits.

....
....
....
....

(3 marks)

Figure 2

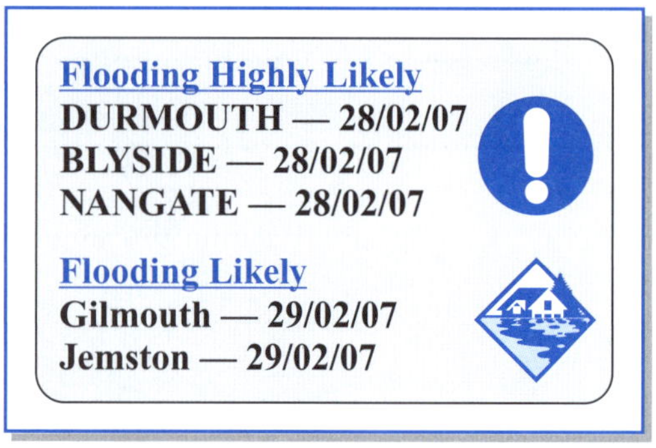

Flooding Highly Likely
DURMOUTH — 28/02/07
BLYSIDE — 28/02/07
NANGATE — 28/02/07

Flooding Likely
Gilmouth — 29/02/07
Jemston — 29/02/07

(c) Study **Figure 2**, which shows an extract from a web page. Describe the costs of the type of strategy shown in **Figure 2**.

The costs are the disadvantages.

....
....
....
....
....

(3 marks)

Unit 1B — Water on the Land

Managing the UK's Water

1   Study **Figure 1** and **Figure 2**, which show rainfall and population density in the UK.

(a) (i) Using **Figure 1** and **Figure 2**, describe the pattern of water supply and demand across the UK.

....

....

....

....

....

....

(2 marks)

Figure 1 — UK average annual rainfall
Key: High, Low

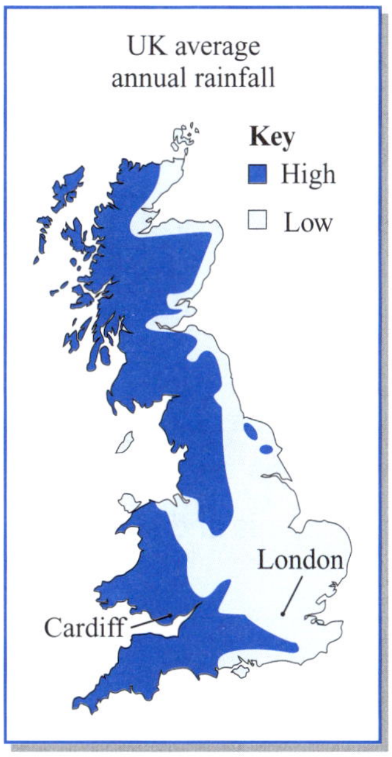

Figure 2 — UK regional population density
Key: Very high, High, Medium, Low

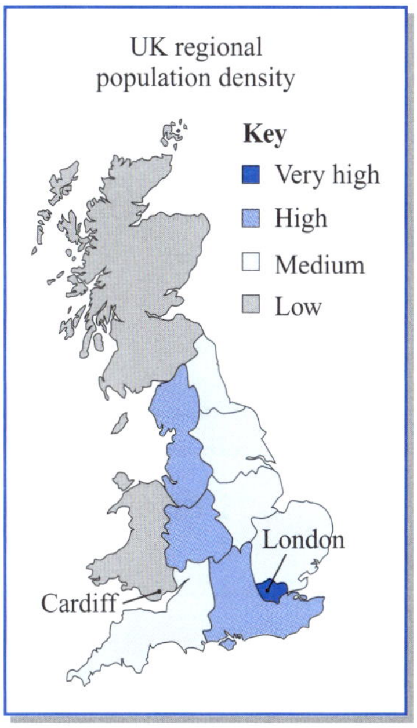

(ii) Are the following places likely to have a water deficit or surplus? Explain your answers.

Cardiff ....

....

London ....

....

(4 marks)

(b) (i) The supply of water can be managed by transferring water from areas of surplus to areas of deficit. Describe two issues that this strategy could cause.

....

....

(2 marks)

(ii) Give two other ways in which the supply of water in the UK can be managed.

....

....

(2 marks)

(c) Describe one way that the demand for water in the UK can be reduced.

....

(1 mark)

2   Describe the economic, social and environmental impacts of a reservoir you have studied.

(8 marks)

Unit 1B — Water on the Land

Unit 1B — Ice on the Land

Ice Levels Over Time

1 Study **Figure 1**, which shows the extent of global ice coverage 20 000 years ago and today.

Figure 1

[Two world maps labelled "20 000 years ago" and "Today", with key showing shaded areas = Ice]

(a) (i) Describe what an ice age is and state what conditions occur during an ice age.

....

....
(2 marks)

(ii) What was the last ice age called?

....
(1 mark)

(b) Using **Figure 1**, compare the distribution of ice on the Earth's surface 20 000 years ago and today.

....

....

....

....

....

....
(6 marks)

> When comparing two distribution maps, you need to describe both of them then say how they're similar and how they're different.

(c) (i) Give two sources of evidence that show changes in global temperature.

....

....
(2 marks)

(ii) For one of these sources, describe and explain how it shows changes in global temperature over time.

....

....
(2 marks)

Glacial Budget

1 Study **Figure 1**, a graph showing how the length of a glacier changed between 1900 and 2000.

(a) (i) Explain the term 'ablation'. On which part of a glacier does most ablation occur?

....

....

....

(2 marks)

Figure 1

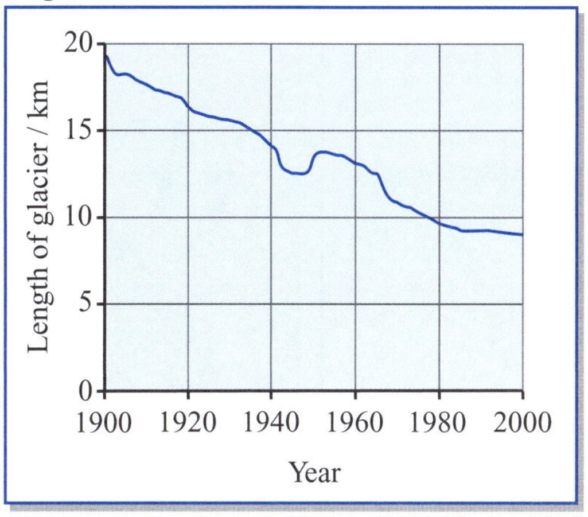

(ii) Explain how the glacial budget affects whether a glacier is advancing or retreating.

....

....

....

....

When you're asked to explain the effect of something always describe what it is first.

....

(6 marks)

(iii) Describe the glacial budget of the glacier shown in **Figure 1**. Explain your answer.

....

....

....

(3 marks)

(iv) By how much did the glacier shown in **Figure 1** decrease in length between 1900 and 2000?

....

(1 mark)

(b) Describe and explain how you would expect the length of a glacier to change over a one year period.

....

....

....

(4 marks)

2 For a retreating glacier you have studied, describe the causes of retreat and the evidence for it.

Remember to put in lots of juicy details when writing about a case study.

(8 marks)

Unit 1B — Ice on the Land

Glacial Erosion

1 Study **Figure 1**, a diagram of a mountainous area where glaciers used to flow.

Figure 1

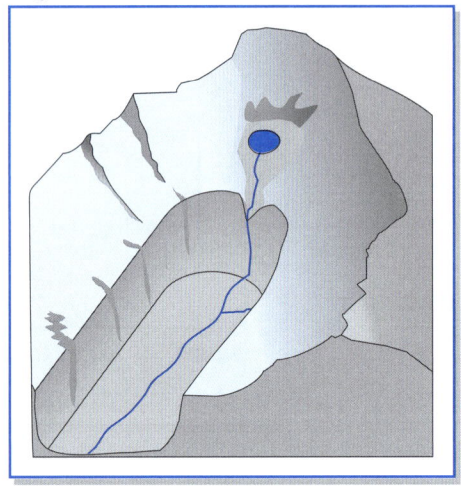

(a) (i) Label the glacial landforms shown in **Figure 1**.

(3 marks)

When labelling a diagram or a photo make sure you draw a line pointing to precisely what you're labelling.

(ii) Describe two ways in which moving ice erodes the landscape.

....
....
....
....

(4 marks)

(b) Explain how the rock above glaciers is weathered.

....
....
....
....

(4 marks)

(c) Study **Figure 2**, a photograph of an Alpine landscape.

(i) Name the glacial landform labelled A in **Figure 2**.

....

(1 mark)

Figure 2

©iStockphoto.com/ Peter Wey

(ii) Explain how this landform is formed.

....

Always double check you've named the right thing in a labelled photograph.

....
....

(3 marks)

Unit 1B — Ice on the Land

Glacial Erosion

2 Study **Figure 3**, an Ordnance Survey® map of part of the Lake District.

Figure 3

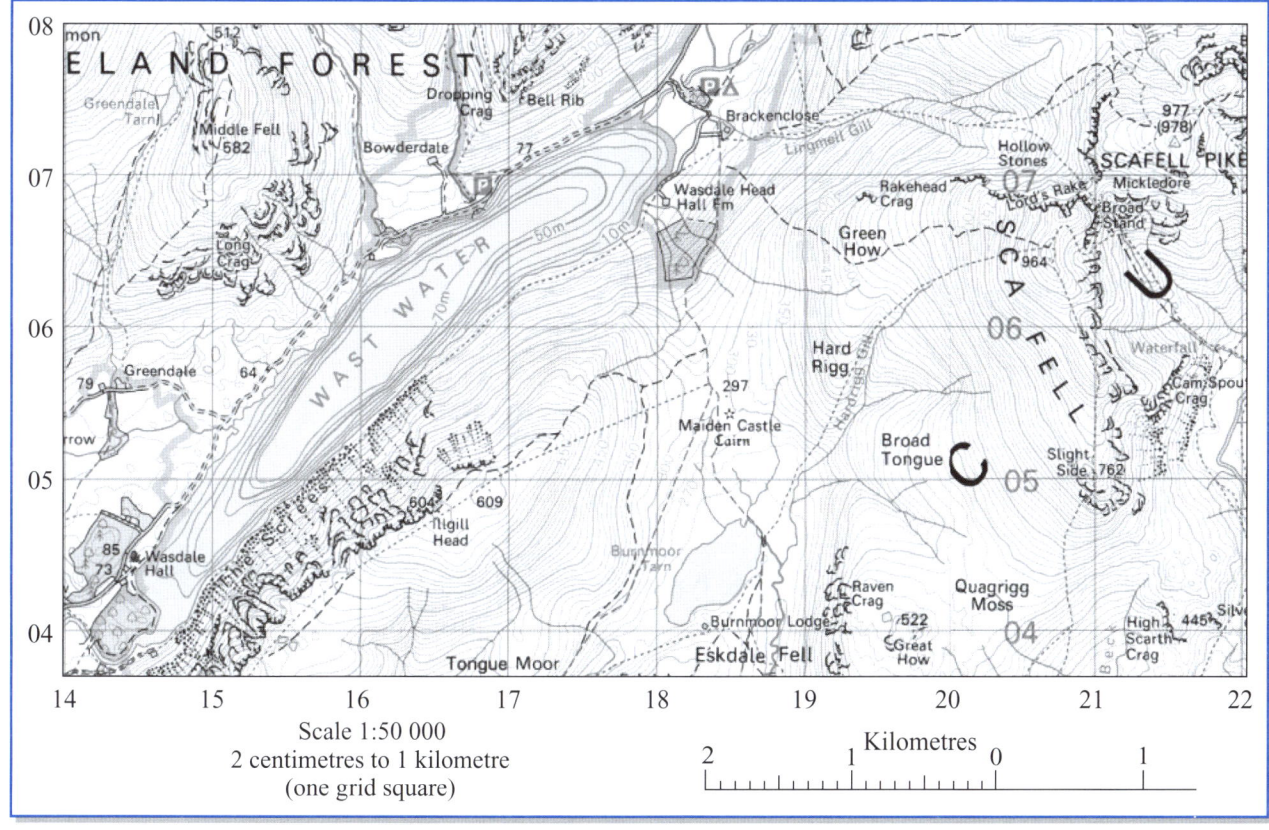

Scale 1:50 000
2 centimetres to 1 kilometre
(one grid square)

(a) There is a truncated spur at grid reference 152065. How are truncated spurs formed?

....
(1 mark)

(b) (i) Name the type of glacial landform found between grid references 146040 and 181072.

....
(1 mark)

(ii) How long is this glacial landform? ....
(1 mark)

Mark the grid references with a cross on the map to help you.

(iii) Describe this type of landform and explain how it is formed.

....

....
(2 marks)

(c) (i) Give the six-figure grid reference for a pyramidal peak shown in **Figure 3**.

....
(1 mark)

(ii) Describe how pyramidal peaks are formed.

....
(1 mark)

Map: Reproduced from Ordnance Survey digital map data © Crown copyright 2001

Unit 1B — Ice on the Land

Glacial Transport and Deposition

1   Study **Figure 1**, a photograph of a glacier.

Figure 1

(a) (i) What is meant by the term 'bulldozing'?

....

....
(1 mark)

(ii) When do glaciers deposit material?

....

....

....

....
(2 marks)

(b) (i) Label **Figure 1** to show the two types of moraine present.
(2 marks)

(ii) Explain the formation of these two types of moraine.

....

....
(2 marks)

(iii) Name two other types of moraine and explain their formation.

....

....

....

....
(4 marks)

(c) **Figure 2** is a sketch map of a drumlin.

Figure 2

(i) Label the sketch map to show the direction of ice flow.
(1 mark)

(ii) Using **Figure 2**, describe the characteristics of a drumlin.

....

....

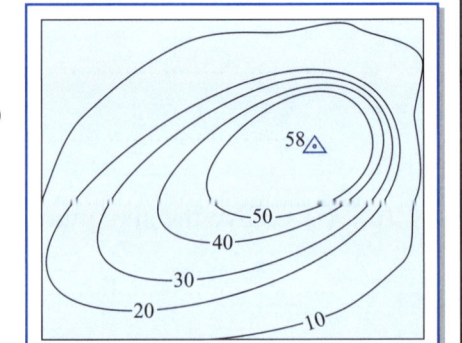

If the question says 'Using Figure 2', you have to quote information from the figure in your answer.

....
(3 marks)

Unit 1B — Ice on the Land

Impacts and Management of Tourism on Ice

1   Study **Figure 1**, a photograph of a ski resort.

   Figure 1

   (a) (i)   Label **Figure 1** to show the economic and environmental impacts
             of tourism on the surrounding area.
   (4 marks)

   (ii) Explain the social impacts of tourism in areas covered in snow and ice.

   ....

   ....

   ....
   (3 marks)

   (b) Describe and explain the strategies used to manage the environmental
       and social impacts of tourism in areas covered in snow and ice.

   > You've talked about some impacts in the questions above, so use those answers to remind you of the strategies to manage them.

   ....

   ....

   ....

   ....

   ....

   ....
   (6 marks)

   (c) For an Alpine area you have studied, describe and explain the attractions for tourists
       and the impacts tourists have on the area.
   (8 marks)

2   For an Alpine area you have studied, describe and explain
    the strategies used to manage tourism in the area. 
   (8 marks)

Unit 1B — Ice on the Land

Impacts of Glacial Retreat

1   Study **Figure 1**, a graph showing annual snowfall and unemployment between 1999 and 2008 in an area covered in snow and ice.

Figure 1

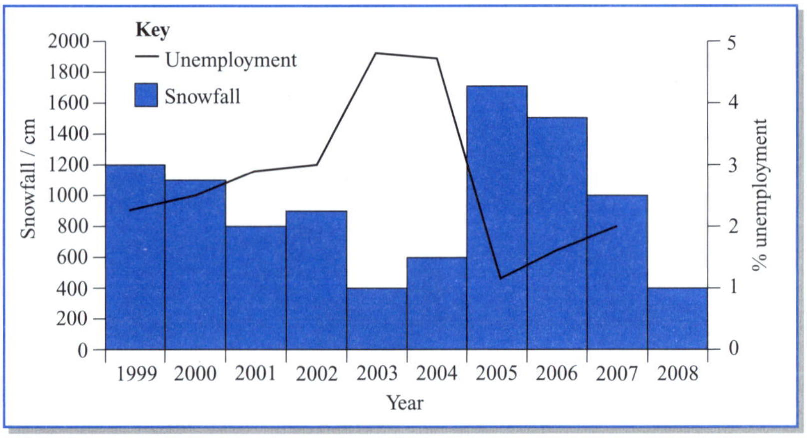

(a) (i)   How much snowfall was there in 2002?

....
(1 mark)

(ii)   Complete the graph to show that unemployment was 4.5% in 2008.

Take care to make your line precise — use a ruler and a sharp pencil.

(1 mark)

(b) (i)   Describe and explain the pattern shown in **Figure 1**.

....

....

....

....
(4 marks)

(ii)   How might glacial retreat affect unemployment?

....

....
(2 marks)

(c)   Describe the social and environmental impacts of unreliable snowfall and glacial retreat.

....

....

....

....

....
(6 marks)

Unit 1B — Ice on the Land

Unit 1B — The Coastal Zone

Coastal Weathering and Erosion

1   Study **Figure 1**, which shows how the coastline of an area has changed over time.

Figure 1

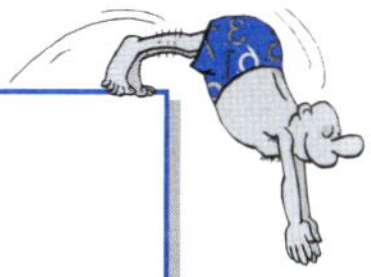

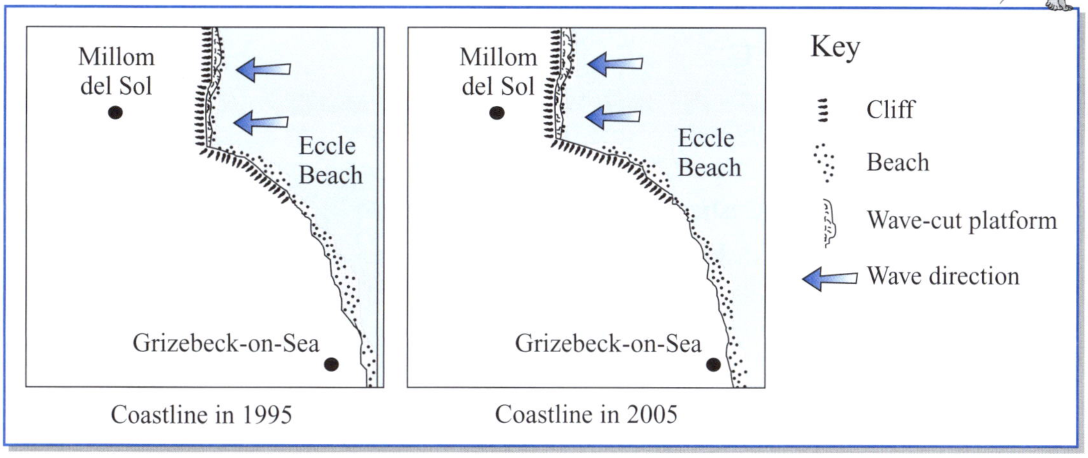

Coastline in 1995 / Coastline in 2005 — showing Millom del Sol, Eccle Beach, Grizebeck-on-Sea

Key: Cliff, Beach, Wave-cut platform, Wave direction

(a) (i)   Name the type of waves shown in **Figure 1**.

   ....
   (1 mark)

   (ii)   Describe the characteristics of these waves.

   ....

   ....

   ....
   (3 marks)

(b)   Name and describe two processes of erosion that act on coastlines.

   ....

   ....

   ....

   ....
   (4 marks)

   It's a four mark question so there are two marks for each process.

(c)   Explain how freeze-thaw weathering causes rock on coastal cliffs to break up.

   ....

   ....

   ....

   ....
   (4 marks)

(d)   What is meant by the term 'mass movement'?

   ....
   (1 mark)

Coastal Landforms Caused by Erosion

1   Study **Figure 1**, a photograph showing coastal landforms.

(a) (i) Name the type of landform labelled A in **Figure 1**.

....
(1 mark)

(ii) Describe the characteristics of the landform labelled A in **Figure 1**.

....

....

....

....
(2 marks)

(iii) Explain how the landforms shown in **Figure 1** are formed.

....

....

....
(3 marks)

(b) Study **Figure 2**, which shows one step in the formation of a wave-cut platform.

(i) Name the features indicated by labels X and Y.

X: ....

Y: ....
(2 marks)

(ii) Using **Figure 2**, explain the formation of wave-cut platforms.

....

....

....

....

....

....
(6 marks)

Unit 1B — The Coastal Zone

Coastal Landforms Caused by Erosion

2 Study **Figure 3**, a photograph of a coastal area.

Figure 3

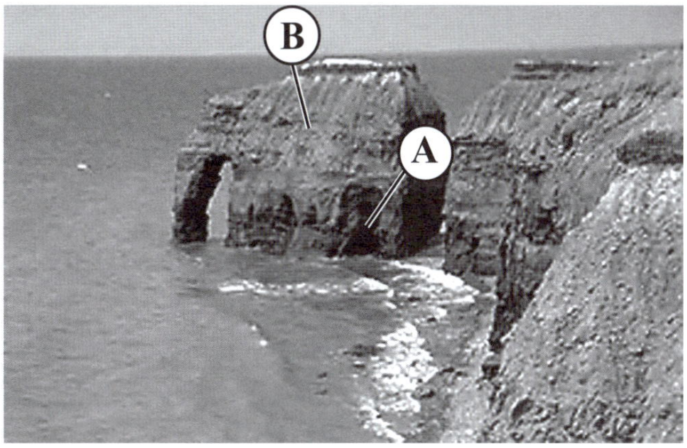

(a) Name the type of landform labelled A in **Figure 3** and explain how it was formed.

....
....
....
....
....

(3 marks)

(b) (i) Label **Figure 3** to show an arch.

(1 mark)

(ii) Explain how an arch is formed.

....
....

(2 marks)

(c) (i) Name the type of landform labelled B in **Figure 3**.

....

(1 mark)

(ii) Describe the characteristics of this landform.

....

(1 mark)

(d) Study **Figure 4**, a photograph of a coastal area. Use evidence from **Figure 4** to suggest what this coastal area may look like in the future. Explain your answer.

Figure 4

....
....
....
....
....
....

For this question you have to describe what the area will look like and explain why.

(3 marks)

Unit 1B — The Coastal Zone

Coastal Transportation and Deposition

1   Study **Figure 1**, a graph showing how the width of a beach varied along its length in the years 2000 and 2005.

(a) (i)   Compare the width of the beach in 2000 with the width in 2005.

....

....

....

....

....

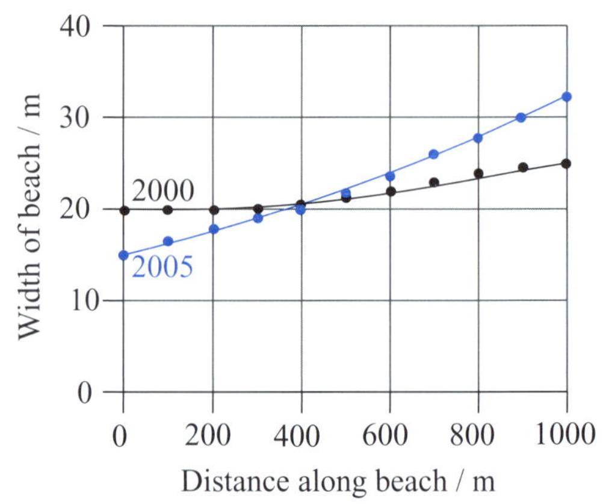

....
(3 marks)

Figure 1

[Graph: Width of beach / m (y-axis, 0–40) vs Distance along beach / m (x-axis, 0–1000). Two lines plotted: 2000 and 2005.]

(ii) The changes in the width of the beach were caused by longshore drift. Describe the process of longshore drift.

....

....

....

....
(4 marks)

(b) Name and describe two other processes of transportation that take place in the sea.

....

....

....

....
(4 marks)

(c) (i)   The total volume of material on the beach increased between 2000 and 2005 because large amounts of material, carried by sea water, were dropped on the coast. What is the name of this process?

....
(1 mark)

(ii) Suggest two factors that affect the amount of material dropped on the coast.

....

....
(2 marks)

Unit 1B — The Coastal Zone

Coastal Landforms Caused by Deposition

1   Study **Figure 1**, an Ordnance Survey® map of a coastal area near Bournemouth.

Figure 1

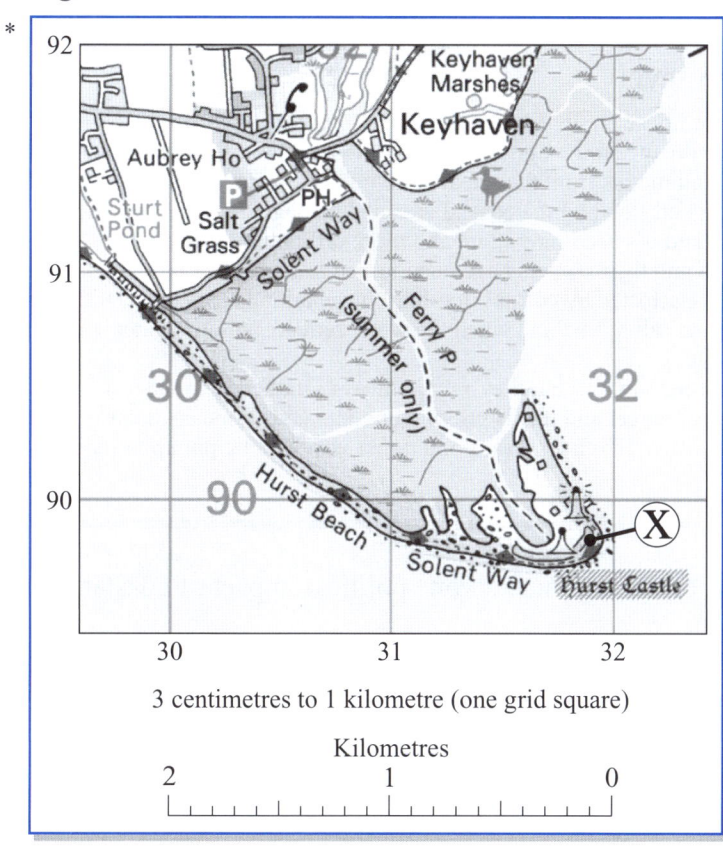

3 centimetres to 1 kilometre (one grid square)

(a) (i) Hurst Castle is found at X on **Figure 1**. Give the six figure grid reference for Hurst Castle.

....
(1 mark)

(ii) State the distance between Hurst Castle and the end of the spit at 316905.

....
(1 mark)

> You'll need to use a ruler and the scale at the bottom of Figure 1 to work this out.

(b) Explain how a spit is formed.

....
....
....
....
(2 marks)

(c) Compare the characteristics of spits and bars.

....
....
....
(3 marks)

(d) **Figure 2** is a picture of a sandy beach.

(i) Describe the characteristics of the beach shown in **Figure 2**.

....
(1 mark)

Figure 2

(ii) Name one other type of beach.

....
(1 mark)

Map: Reproduced from Ordnance Survey digital map data © Crown copyright 2001

Unit 1B — The Coastal Zone

Rising Sea Level and Coastal Flooding

1. Study **Figure 1**, a news article about the effects of rising sea level on Australia.

    Figure 1

    > **The rising costs of rising sea level**
    >
    > The idea of living in a multi-million dollar house on the Sydney coast may seem like a dream lifestyle, but for many people living in the area the dream shows signs of turning into a nightmare. Rising sea level means that houses that used to be a hundred metres from the sea are now just a few metres away.
    > In stormy weather the water rises even higher, flooding the coastal area and damaging many properties. The cost of repairing this damage is high and it's becoming more and more difficult to insure houses in the area. Some houses cannot be repaired and their owners have been forced to leave their homes and move elsewhere. And it's not just houses that are affected by coastal flooding. Vegetation is damaged and land is eroded by the influx of sea water, whilst the salt left behind when the water retreats pollutes water supplies and leaves farmland unusable.
    > Residents are turning to local government for support, but they're not always satisfied with the response. The policy in some areas is to allow coastal retreat and this is proving unpopular, as it means many people will have to leave their homes and move away. In other areas, flood defences are being put up to try and tackle the problems of rising sea level.

    (a) Using **Figure 1**, describe one social, one economic and one political impact of coastal flooding.

    Social..
    ....
    Economic..
    ....
    Political..
    ....

    Only write about the impacts mentioned in Figure 1.

    (3 marks)

    (b) Suggest two ways that coastal flooding can impact on the environment.

    ....
    ....

    (2 marks)

    (c) Rising sea level is caused by global warming.
    Explain two ways that global warming causes sea level to rise.

    ....
    ....
    ....
    ....

    (4 marks)

    (d) Describe the impacts of coastal flooding on an area you have studied.

    (8 marks)

Unit 1B — The Coastal Zone

Coastal Erosion

1. Study **Figure 1**, a sketch map of the Sparkington coastal area.

   Figure 1

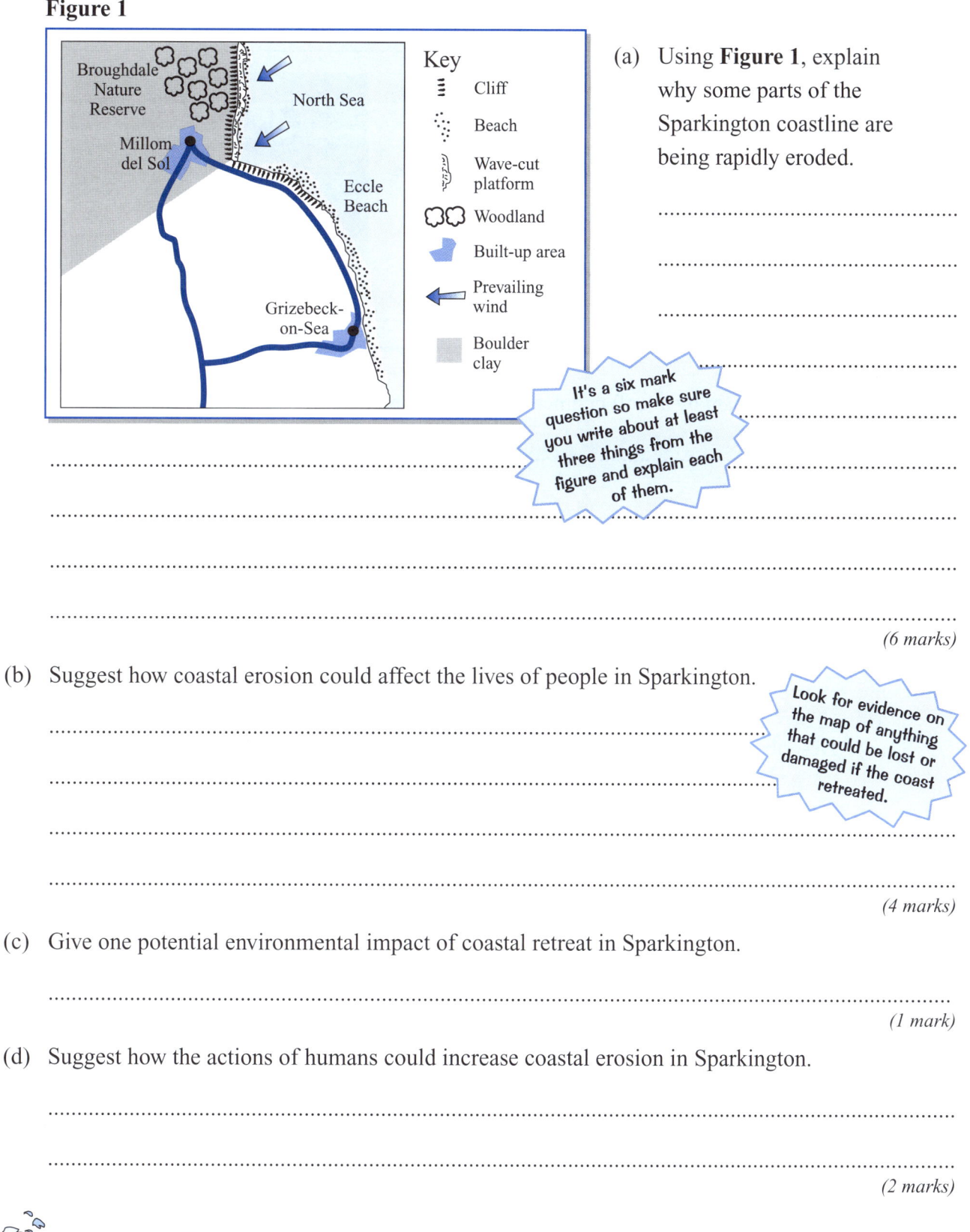

   (a) Using **Figure 1**, explain why some parts of the Sparkington coastline are being rapidly eroded.

   ....
   ....
   ....
   ....
   ....
   ....

   It's a six mark question so make sure you write about at least three things from the figure and explain each of them.

   ....
   ....
   ....
   ....
   (6 marks)

   (b) Suggest how coastal erosion could affect the lives of people in Sparkington.

   Look for evidence on the map of anything that could be lost or damaged if the coast retreated.

   ....
   ....
   ....
   ....
   (4 marks)

   (c) Give one potential environmental impact of coastal retreat in Sparkington.

   ....
   (1 mark)

   (d) Suggest how the actions of humans could increase coastal erosion in Sparkington.

   ....
   ....
   (2 marks)

2. Describe the impacts of coastal erosion on a coastal area you have studied.

   (8 marks)

Unit 1B — The Coastal Zone

Coastal Management Strategies

1   Study **Figure 1**, a news article about coastal defences in Cliffall, a UK coastal town.

Figure 1

> **Hope for Cliffall's coastline**
>
> Work is due to start next week on new defences for the Cliffall coastline. The town has been suffering from the effects of coastal erosion over the last few years but it's hoped the new defences will prevent further problems. The scheme will use a combination of defences, including groynes, dune regeneration and beach nourishment. The work will be completed gradually over the next four years, with the groynes the top priority.

(a) (i) What is meant by a 'soft engineering' coastal defence?

....
(1 mark)

(ii) Name one soft engineering strategy mentioned in **Figure 1**.

....
(1 mark)

(b) (i) Describe one benefit of a soft engineering strategy mentioned in **Figure 1**.

....
(1 mark)

(ii) Describe any disadvantages of using this strategy as a method of coastal defence.

....

....
(2 marks)

(c) (i) Name and describe one hard engineering strategy not mentioned in **Figure 1** that could be used to protect the coastline.

....

....
(2 marks)

(ii) Explain the advantages of using this strategy as a coastal defence.

....

....
(2 marks)

(d) Explain the benefits and costs of coastal management strategies used in an area you have studied.

(8 marks)

Coastal Habitat

1 Study **Figure 1**, an article about mangrove forests.

Figure 1

Mangrove Forests

Mangrove forests are found on tropical and subtropical coasts, in areas where saline (salty) seawater mixes with freshwater from the land. Mangrove trees are adapted to this environment as they have roots that can filter salt out of water.
The forests are home to many species of birds, animals and fish. In fact, up to 75% of tropical fish use mangroves for food, shelter or breeding grounds.

Mangrove forests are also important to humans — providing protection from coastal erosion, flooding, and storm surges. Unfortunately, large areas of mangrove forest are at risk from human activities such as urban development, shrimp farming, pollution, over-fishing and deforestation. For example, the Indus Delta in Pakistan, which has 1600 square km of mangrove forest, provides wood for fuel and fishing grounds for over 100 000 people.

Conservation strategies have been implemented to limit the damage caused by these activities. Strategies include increasing the availability of alternatives to wood for fuel and limiting the mesh size of fishing nets, which prevents smaller fish being caught before they've had a chance to breed. It's hoped that these conservation strategies will help the forests survive well into the future.

(a) Using evidence from **Figure 1**, suggest why it is important to conserve mangrove forests.

....

....
(2 marks)

(b) (i) Explain why there is a conflict between land uses in the Indus Delta.

....

....
(2 marks)

(ii) Explain how the conservation strategies described in **Figure 1** could allow the area to be used sustainably.

The question asks you to explain so don't forget to say why the strategies help.

....

....

....

....
(4 marks)

(c) Describe the environmental characteristics and the wildlife of a coastal habitat you have studied.
(8 marks)

(d) Explain the strategies that have been implemented to allow the sustainable use of a coastal habitat you have studied. 
(8 marks)

Unit 1B — The Coastal Zone

Unit 2A — Population Change

Population Growth

1 Study **Figure 1**, which shows world population for the years 1500-2000.

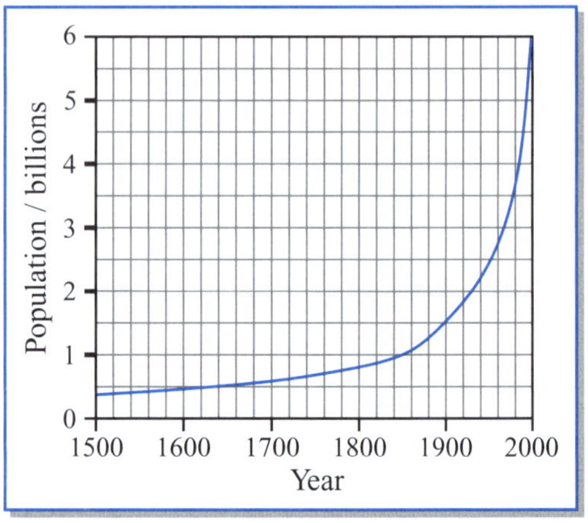

(a) (i) What was the world population in 1900?

....
(1 mark)

Figure 1

(ii) How many years did it take for the world population to double from 1 billion to 2 billion people?

....
(1 mark)

(b) Birth rate affects the population size of the world. Define the term 'birth rate'.

....
(1 mark)

2 Study **Figure 2**, which shows the Demographic Transition Model (DTM).

Figure 2

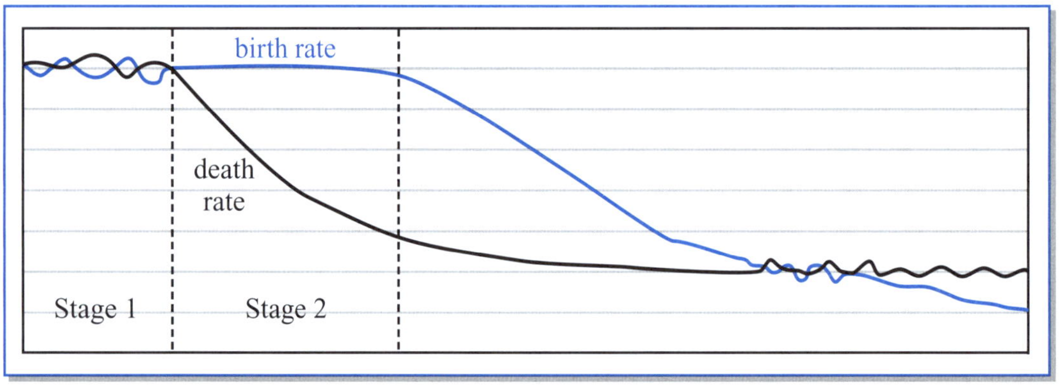

(a) Add dotted lines and labels to **Figure 2** to show when Stages 3, 4 and 5 occur.
(1 mark)

Use a pencil to draw lines so you can change them if you need to.

(b) (i) Using **Figure 2**, compare the death rate and birth rate of a country in Stage 1 with a country in Stage 2.

....

....
(2 marks)

(ii) How does the size of the population change between Stages 1 and 2?

....
(1 mark)

(c) Yemen is a country in south west Asia that is poorer and less developed than the UK. Is Yemen likely to be in an earlier or a later stage of the DTM than the UK?

....
(1 mark)

Unit 2A — Population Change

Population Growth and Structure

1 Study **Figures 1a**, **1b** and **1c**, which show population pyramids for countries A, B and C.

Figure 1a — Country A **Figure 1b — Country B** 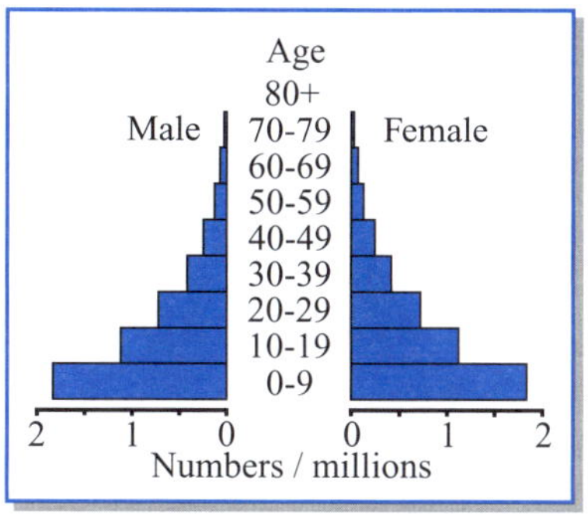 **Figure 1c — Country C**

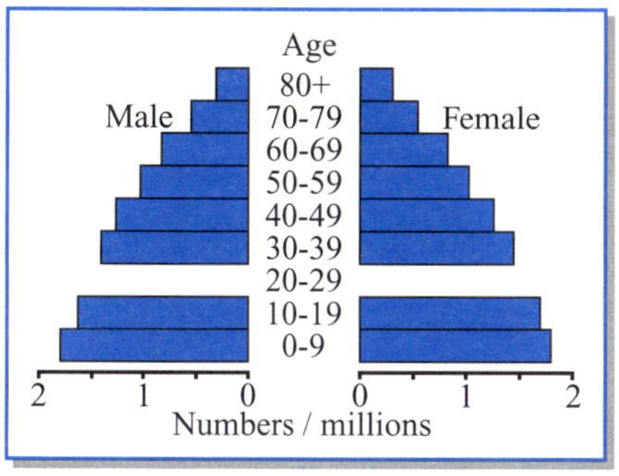

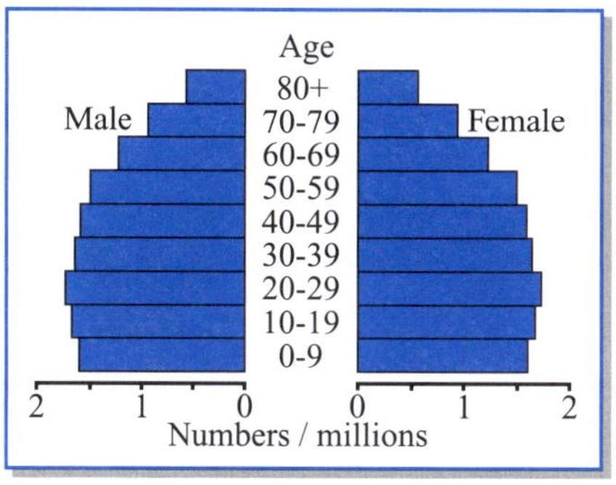

(a) What do population pyramids show?

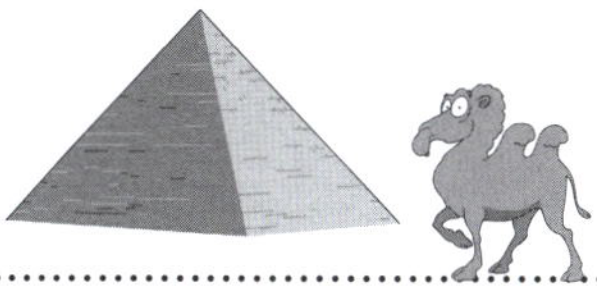

....

....

(2 marks)

(b) Complete **Figure 1a** to show that the population of Country A includes 1.6 million women aged 20-29, and 1.5 million men aged 20-29.

(1 mark)

(c) Compare the population pyramids for Country A and Country B.

....

....

....

....

....

....

Compare means you should talk about the similarities and differences.

(6 marks)

(d) Suggest which stage of the DTM Country C is in. Give reasons for your answer.

....

....

(3 marks)

(e) Birth rate rapidly falls in Stage 3 of the DTM. Suggest reasons for why this happens.

....

....

....

(3 marks)

Unit 2A — Population Change

Managing Rapid Population Growth

1   Study **Figure 1**, which shows how the population changed in the region of Thirton between 1960 and 2000.

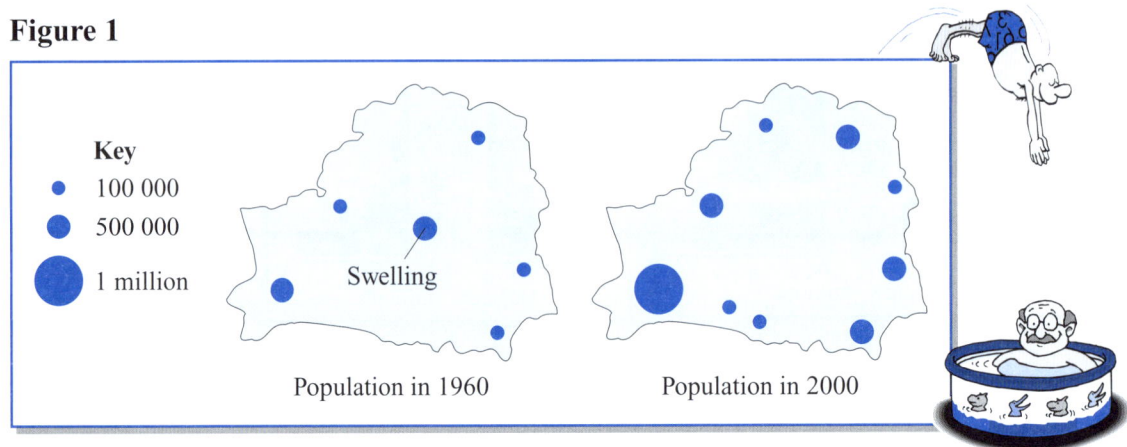

Figure 1

Key
- 100 000
- 500 000
- 1 million

Swelling

Population in 1960   Population in 2000

(a) (i) Complete **Figure 1** to show that the city of Swelling had a population of 1 million in 2000.
(1 mark)

(ii) Use **Figure 1** to describe how the population of Thirton changed between 1960 and 2000.

....

....
(2 marks)

(b) Rapid population growth has many impacts on a country. Describe two social and two economic impacts of rapid population growth.

> The question asks for social and economic impacts so don't put in any political impacts.

....

....

....

....
(4 marks)

(c) Describe a population policy that could help to address rapid population growth and explain whether or not the policy helps to achieve sustainable development.

....

....

....

....
(4 marks)

2   Compare the policies used in China to control rapid population growth with the policies used in one other named country.

(8 marks)
spelling, punctuation and grammar: 3 marks

Unit 2A — Population Change

Managing Ageing Populations

1 Study **Figure 1**, which shows the population pyramid of a country.

(a) (i) Which age range contains the largest number of men?

....
(1 mark)

Figure 1

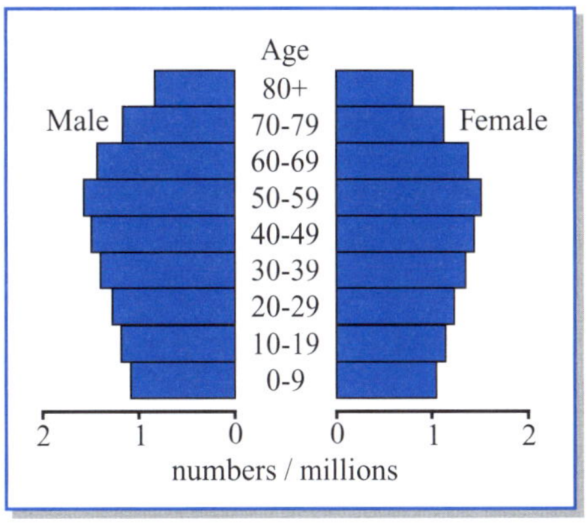

[Population pyramid showing Male/Female by age groups: 0-9, 10-19, 20-29, 30-39, 40-49, 50-59, 60-69, 70-79, 80+; numbers/millions axis from 2 to 0 to 2]

(ii) Use evidence from **Figure 1** to describe the population structure of the country.

....

....

The question's only worth 2 marks so your answer should be brief.

....
(2 marks)

(b) (i) Suggest which stage of the Demographic Transition Model a country with a population structure like that shown in **Figure 1** would be in.

....
(1 mark)

(ii) Name a country with a population structure similar to that shown in **Figure 1**.

....
(1 mark)

(c) Explain what effect a population structure like the one in **Figure 1** may have on a country's birth rate.

....

....
(2 marks)

(d) Ageing populations have lots of impacts which can affect the development of a country. Describe the social and economic impacts of an ageing population.

....

....

Old people rule

....

....

....

....
(6 marks)

Unit 2A — Population Change

Managing Ageing Populations

2 Study **Figure 2**, which shows how the population of Country A (a nation with an ageing population) has changed between 1960 and 2008.

Figure 2

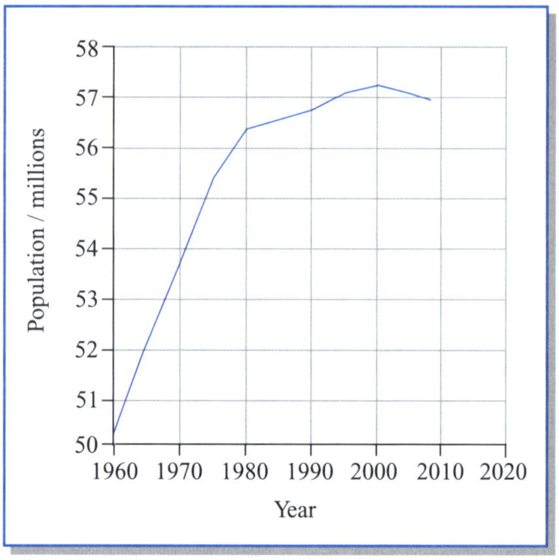

(a) (i) Use **Figure 2** to describe how the population of Country A changed between 1960 and 2008.

....

....

....

....
(2 marks)

(ii) Complete **Figure 2** to show that Country A is predicted to have a population of 57.8 million in the year 2015.
(1 mark)

(b) (i) Women in Country A are offered cash incentives to have more children. Explain why this strategy may help to reduce the problems caused by an ageing population.

....

....
(2 marks)

(ii) Explain whether this strategy helps towards sustainable development.

....

....
(2 marks)

(c) Suggest another strategy besides offering cash incentives that could be used to manage Country A's population and explain whether the strategy helps towards sustainable development or not.

....

....
(2 marks)

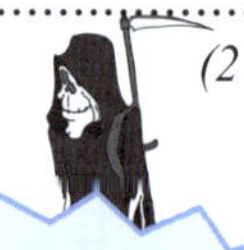

3 Choose one country in the European Union with an ageing population.

Name of Country ....

Explain why this country has an ageing population and describe the strategies that are being used to cope with the ageing population.

(8 marks)
spelling, punctuation and grammar: 3 marks

> Read the question carefully. Here you need to write about a country in the EU, not any old country.

Unit 2A — Population Change

Population Movements

1   Study **Figure 1**, which shows some of the yearly immigration to the UK, averaged over the period 1996-2000.

Figure 1

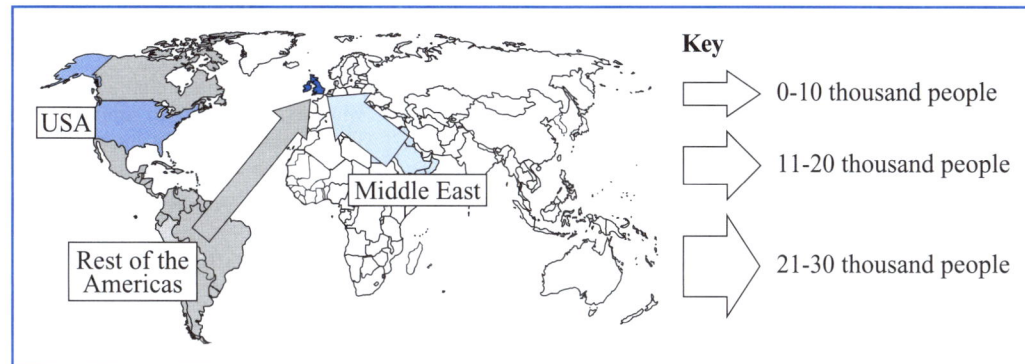

Key:
- 0-10 thousand people
- 11-20 thousand people
- 21-30 thousand people

(a) (i) What is immigration?

....
(1 mark)

(ii) How many people migrated to the UK from the Middle East?

....
(1 mark)

(iii) Complete **Figure 1** by adding an arrow to show that immigration to the UK from the USA was 29 600 people.

Use a ruler to get the width of the arrow exactly right.

(1 mark)

(b) Suggest the impacts that migration to the UK might have on the UK.

....

....
(2 marks)

(c) Describe the negative impacts that immigration can have on a source country.

....

....

....
(3 marks)

(d) Migration happens because of push and pull factors. Describe what push and pull factors are.

....

It's always a good idea to give examples in your answer even if the question doesn't ask for them.

....

....
(4 marks)

Unit 2A — Population Change

Migration Within and To the EU

1 Study **Figure 1**, an extract from a report into migration from Poland to the UK.

(a) (i) Using **Figure 1**, suggest two push factors that might have caused Polish people to migrate to the UK.

Figure 1

> Between 2004 and 2007 it's estimated that more than half a million Poles migrated to the UK. The reasons for migration vary from person to person, but most Polish immigrants are thought to be economic migrants who wanted to work to support their family in Poland. Unlike most EU countries, the UK doesn't have a limit to the number of immigrants it will accept from Poland.

....
....
(2 marks)

(ii) Suggest one other push factor that might cause people to migrate.

....
(1 marks)

(b) Using **Figure 1**, suggest two pull factors that caused Polish people to migrate to the UK.

....
....
(2 marks)

2 Study **Figure 2**, which shows the number of refugees in France and the Netherlands from 2001 to 2006.

(a) (i) What are refugees?

....
(1 mark)

Figure 2

Year	France	Netherlands
2001	131 601	151 928
2002	132 182	148 362
2003	130 838	140 886
2004	139 852	126 805
2005	137 316	118 189
2006	145 996	100 574

(ii) Between which years did refugee numbers in the Netherlands fall the most?

....
(1 mark)

(iii) Using **Figure 2**, describe how the refugee population of France changed from 2001 to 2006.

The question says 'Using Figure 2' so make sure you quote some figures from the table.

....
....
....
(4 marks)

(b) Explain why the refugees might have left their country of origin.

....
....
(2 marks)

(c) For a refugee migration to the EU you have studied, describe the impacts on the source countries and the receiving countries.
(8 marks)
spelling, punctuation and grammar: 3 marks

Unit 2A — Population Change

Unit 2A — Changing Urban Environments

Urbanisation

1. Study **Figure 1**, which shows the population growth of Pieville, a city in a rich country.

    Figure 1

    (a) (i) The population of Pieville is predicted to reach 65 000 in 2025. Complete the graph by plotting this figure.
    (1 mark)

    When you're completing a graph, keep it neat and readable — use a ruler, mark points with a sharp pencil, join the dots and then check it's right.

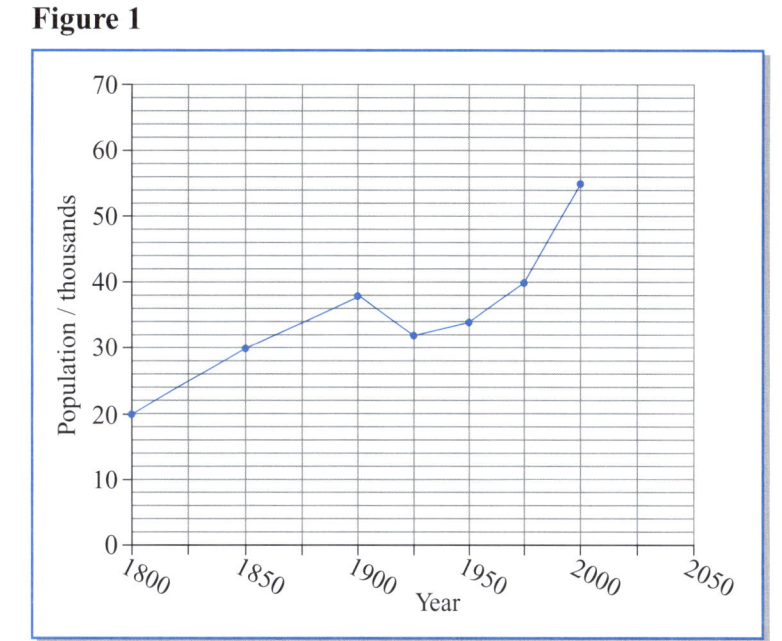

    (ii) Use **Figure 1** to describe how the population of Pieville changed between 1800 and 2000.

    ....
    ....
    ....
    (3 marks)

    (b) Population change in Pieville was affected by rural-urban migration between 1800 and 1900.

    (i) What is meant by the term 'rural-urban migration'?

    ....
    (1 mark)

    (ii) Suggest why there was an increase in rural-urban migration in richer countries between 1800 and 1900.

    ....
    ....
    (2 marks)

    (iii) Suggest reasons for rural-urban migration in poorer countries.

    ....
    ....
    (2 marks)

    (iv) Other than rural-urban migration, give two further causes of urbanisation.

    ....
    ....
    (2 marks)

Unit 2A — Changing Urban Environments

Parts of a City

1. Study **Figures 1** and **2**. **Figure 1** shows two photographs from different parts of a city. **Figure 2** is a model of a typical city viewed from above, which shows roughly where the four different parts of a city are located.

   Figure 1

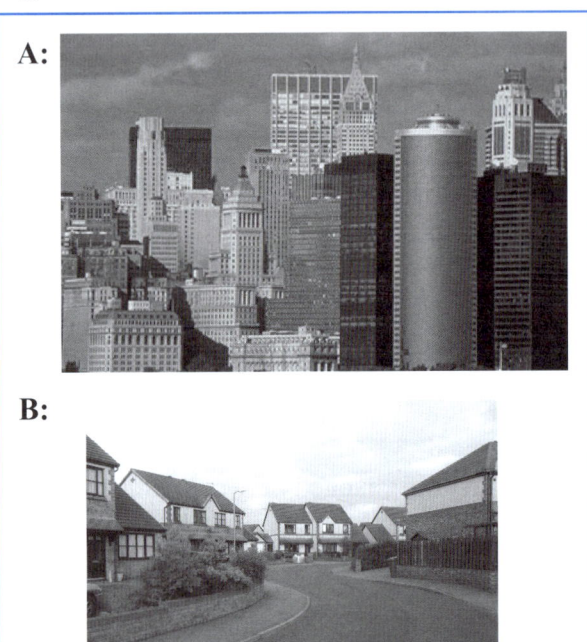

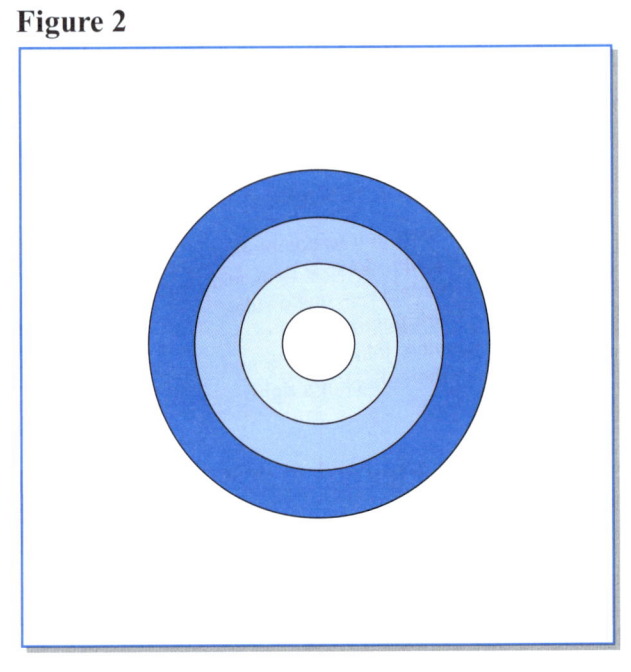

   A:

   B:

   Figure 2

   (a) (i) Name the parts of the city shown in the photos in **Figure 1**.

   Photo A: .... Photo B: ....
   (2 marks)

   (ii) Label **Figure 2** to show where you would expect each of these parts to be found.
   (2 marks)

   (b) For a city in a richer country, describe the typical land use of:

   the inner city...

   ....

   the rural-urban fringe..

   ....
   (4 marks)

   (c) Suggest ways in which the land use in a city could vary over time.

   ....

   ....

   ....
   (3 marks)

Unit 2A — Changing Urban Environments

Urban Issues

1. Study **Figure 1**, which shows state-provided housing statistics for Looptown, a city in a rich country.

   Figure 1

Year	Population	State housing available	No. of people on housing list
1980	26 000	10 000	2000
1990	37 000	9000	12 000
2000	49 000	7500	23 000

   (a) (i) How many more people were on the housing list in 2000 than in 1990?

   ....
   (1 mark)

   (ii) How can housing shortages in rich countries be tackled?

   ....
   ....
   ....
   ....
   (4 marks)

   (b) Study **Figure 2**, which shows the city centre of Looptown before and after redevelopment.

   Figure 2 — Before redevelopment / After redevelopment

   (i) Why do some CBDs in rich countries suffer from decline?

   ....
   ....
   ....
   ....
   ....
   (2 marks)

   (ii) Use evidence from **Figure 2** to describe how the city centre has been redeveloped.

   Look for any obvious differences between the two pictures.

   ....
   ....
   ....
   ....
   (4 marks)

   (c) Suggest one effect that government investment might have on a run-down city centre.

   ....
   (1 mark)

Unit 2A — Changing Urban Environments

Urban Issues

2 Study **Figure 2**, which shows some transport statistics for an urban area.

(a) (i) How many serious traffic accidents were there in 1990?

....
(1 mark)

Figure 2

(ii) Describe and explain the correlation between car ownership and serious traffic accidents.

Correlation means the relationship between two or more things.

....
....
....
....
(2 marks)

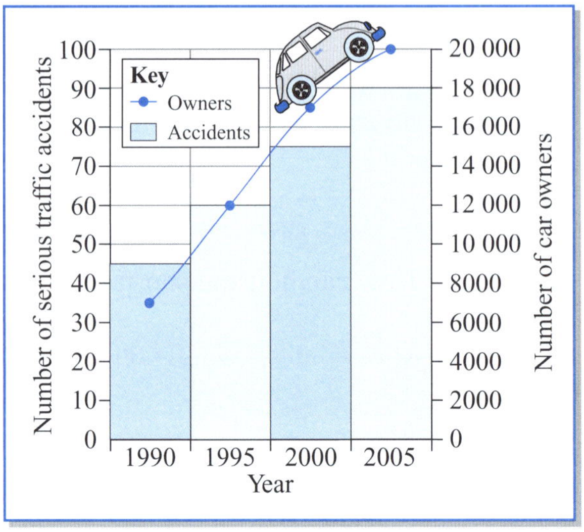

(b) Describe a strategy that could help reduce car use in urban areas.

....
....
(2 marks)

3 Study **Figure 3**, which shows the percentage of people speaking different first languages in areas of Dumblewood City.

Figure 3

	First language			
Area	English	Welsh	Hindi	Polish
Trumpetville	70	12	8	10
Watertown	36	18	24	22
Sproutington	54	16	7	23

(a) Are there signs of ethnic segregation in Dumblewood City? Use evidence from **Figure 3** to support your answer.

....
....
....
(2 marks)

(b) Give one cause of ethnic segregation within urban areas.

....
(1 mark)

(c) Describe how Dumblewood Council could support the multicultural nature of the city.

....
....
(2 marks)

Squatter Settlements

1   Study **Figure 1**, a photo of a squatter settlement, and **Figure 2**, an article about the settlement.

Figure 1

Figure 2

Zorbi squatter settlement has increased in size in the last 10 years. The few services that exist aren't enough for the population, and there is currently no healthcare or policing within the settlement. Some work is available but it is low paid and the hours are long. However, the government is developing Site and Service schemes to help residents and improve community spirit.

(a) (i)   What is meant by the term 'squatter settlement'?

....
(1 mark)

(ii) Use **Figure 1** to describe the characteristics of a squatter settlement.

....

....

....
(3 marks)

(iii) Use **Figures 1** and **2** to help you describe life in a squatter settlement.

....

....

....

....

....
(4 marks)

Use evidence from the Figures and what you've learnt in class to answer questions like this.

(b) Explain why squatter settlements develop in some cities in poorer countries.

....

....
(2 marks)

(c) Describe how Site and Service schemes work.

....

....
(2 marks)

Unit 2A — Changing Urban Environments

Squatter Settlements

2 Study **Figure 3**, which is an extract from a website promoting the Can-Can Squatter Settlement Redevelopment Project.

Figure 3

The Can-Can Squatter Settlement Redevelopment Project started in 1991 to help improve life for Zorbi residents. The project involves self-help and local authority schemes including the installation of a sewage disposal system. The project also aims to improve quality of life by improving healthcare and education.

Year	Literacy rate	% people in work	% people with access to clean water	No. of people per doctor	Average life expectancy
1980	3%	27	33	2000	49
1990	3%	26	36	2000	49
2000	37%	69	73	500	57

(a) (i) Use evidence from **Figure 3** to describe the success of the Can-Can project.

....

When describing the success of a project, you need to use evidence to back up your statements.

....

....

....

....

....

(6 marks)

(ii) Suggest one reason why the percentage of people with access to clean water increased between 1990 and 2000.

....

(1 mark)

(b) Describe how a self-help scheme can improve life in squatter settlements.

....

....

(2 marks)

(c) What are local authority schemes?

....

....

(1 mark)

3 Describe a redevelopment project in a squatter settlement you have studied. How successful has the project been?

(8 marks)
spelling, punctuation and grammar: 3 marks

Unit 2A — Changing Urban Environments

Urbanisation — Environmental Issues

1   Study **Figure 1**, which shows some statistics for a city in a poor country.

(a) (i) The population rose to 1.9 million people in the year 2000. Complete the graph to show this.
(1 mark)

(ii) The number of factories quadrupled from 1960 to 1980. Complete the graph to show this.
(1 mark)

Figure 1

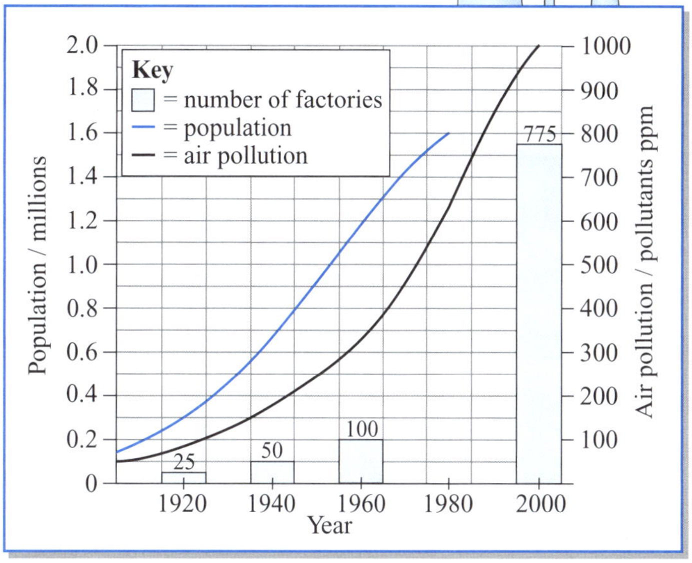

(b) (i) Use **Figure 1** to describe and explain the correlation between urbanisation and air pollution.

Always read the key and graph axes carefully, especially when graphs show a lot of data.

....
....
....
....
(3 marks)

(ii) Explain how industrialisation affects air pollution.

....
....
(2 marks)

(c) (i) Describe the environmental effects of air pollution.

....
....
(2 marks)

(ii) Suggest ways that air pollution can be managed.

....
....
(2 marks)

(d) One of the main effects of urbanisation is the generation of large amounts of waste. Explain why dealing with the disposal of waste is harder for poorer countries.

....
....
....
(3 marks)

Unit 2A — Changing Urban Environments

Sustainable Cities

1 In 2000, Doolally City introduced a policy to encourage sustainable living.
Study **Figure 1**, which shows some Doolally statistics before and after introducing the policy.

(a) (i) How many new houses were built in 2005?

....
(1 mark)

(ii) How many extra recycling sites were created between 1995 and 2005?

....
(1 mark)

Figure 1

Air pollution / pollutants ppm vs Year (1995, 2005)

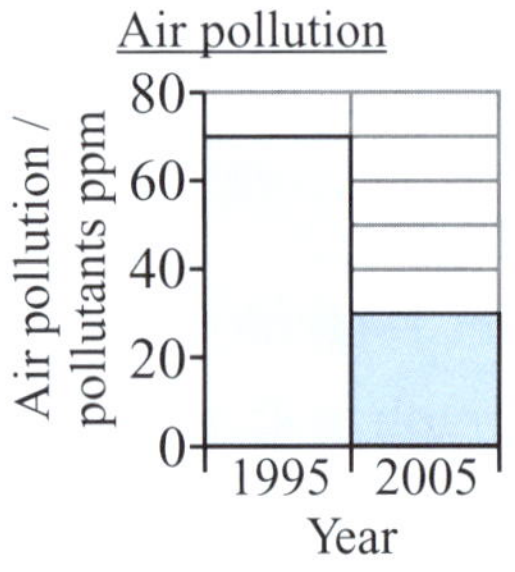

Housing
Year	New housing built
1995	🏠🏠
2005	🏠🏠🏠

Key: 🏠 = 500 new houses

Recycling
Year	No. recycling sites
1995									
2005																							

Transport use — 1995, 2005

Key: = car, = bus, = cycle, = tram, = hydrogen bus

There's a lot of information in Figure 1 so read it carefully before starting your answer.

(b) What is meant by the term 'sustainable living'?

....
....
....
....
(1 mark)

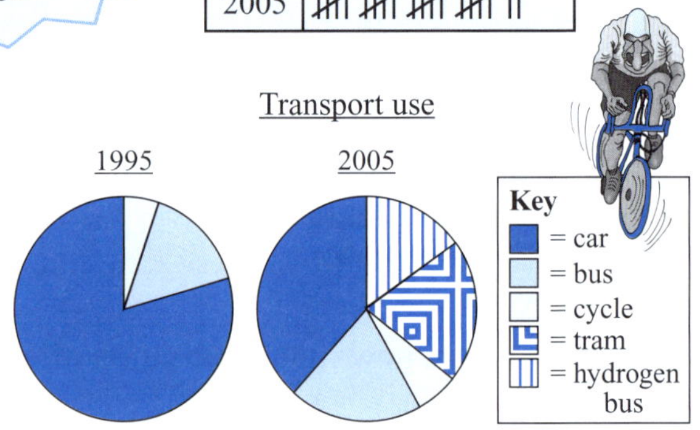

(c) (i) Describe how the changes to transport use shown in **Figure 1** mean Doolally is becoming a more sustainable city.

....
....
....
(3 marks)

(ii) Use **Figure 1** to explain one other way in which Doolally is trying to be more sustainable.

....
....
(2 marks)

(d) Describe how new housing can be built in a sustainable way.

....
....
(2 marks)

2 Using a named example, describe an attempt at sustainable urban living. How successful has this attempt been?

(8 marks)
spelling, punctuation and grammar: 3 marks

Unit 2A — Changing Urban Environments

Unit 2A — Changing Rural Environments

Change in the Rural-Urban Fringe

1   Study **Figure 1**, which shows an area of Byrnshire in 1950 and 2009.

Figure 1

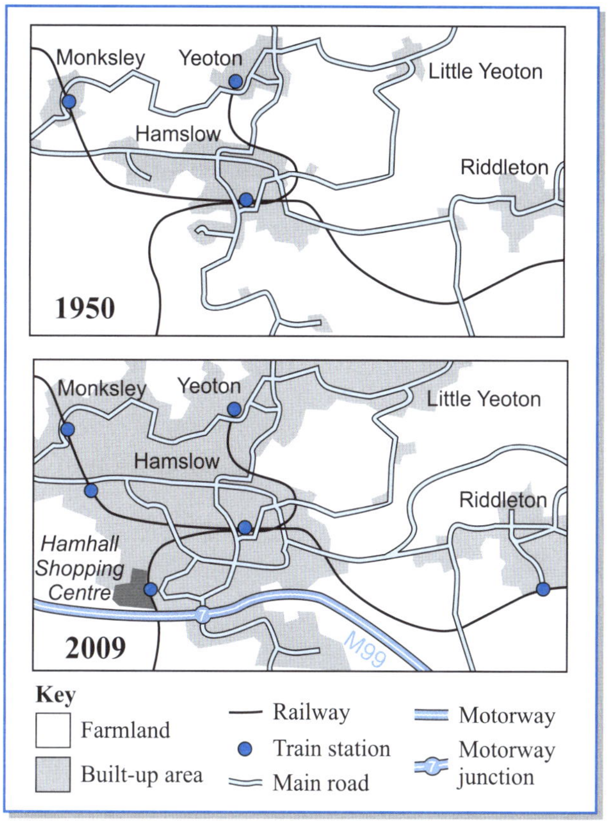

(a) (i) Using **Figure 1**, describe how the rural-urban fringe around Hamslow has changed between 1950 and 2009.

....

....

....

....

....

....

(4 marks)

(ii) Describe and explain the impacts these changes may have had on the rural-urban fringe.

....

....

....

....

(4 marks)

(b) (i) Riddleton is a commuter village on the outskirts of Hamslow. What is a commuter village?

....

(1 mark)

(ii) Suggest reasons why Riddleton increased in size.

> Use the information you've already been given — that Riddleton is a commuter village — to help you answer the question. The question's basically, "Why do commuter villages get bigger?" in disguise.

....

....

....

(2 marks)

(iii) Give two common characteristics of growing villages.

....

....

(2 marks)

Change in Rural Areas

1 Study **Figure 1**, which shows how the population of Bumbleside, a rural village, has changed between 1950 and 2000.

Figure 1

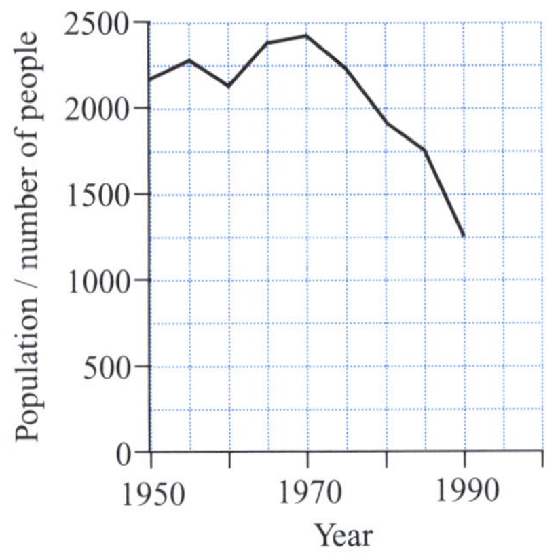

(a) What was the population of Bumbleside in 1985?

....
(1 mark)

(b) Complete **Figure 1** to show that the population of Bumbleside was 1000 in the year 1995 and 500 in 2000.
(2 marks)

(c) (i) Describe how the population of Bumbleside changed between 1970 and 2000.

....

....
(1 mark)

(ii) In 1970, a nearby mine closed. Explain how this may have caused the population change.

....

....

....
(3 marks)

2 Study **Figure 2**, an advert for a house for sale in a rural village.

Figure 2

Sunnyside cottage

A charming converted barn located in Loreton, a small peaceful village popular with second home owners.

Set in stunning countryside, shops and other amenities are just a 30 minute drive away. Note: Public transport is limited in this area — own car recommended.

(a) Loreton is a declining village. Using the information in **Figure 2** and your own knowledge, describe two characteristics of declining villages.

....

....
(2 marks)

(b) A high percentage of the houses in Loreton are second homes.
Explain how this could have contributed to there being no shops in the village.

....

....

....
(3 marks)

3 Describe the causes and impacts of depopulation of a named rural area in the UK.
(8 marks)
spelling, punctuation and grammar: 3 marks

Unit 2A — Changing Rural Environments

Change in UK Commercial Farming

1   Study **Figure 1**, showing the use of an area of agricultural land in 1950 and in 2000.

Figure 1

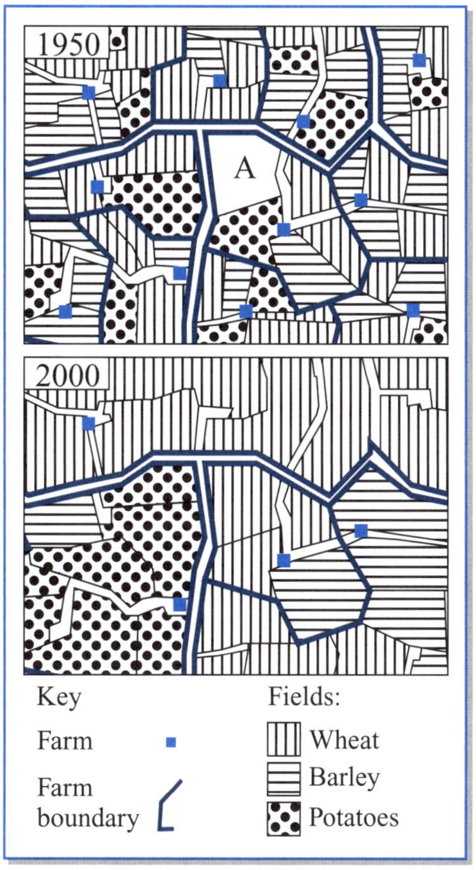

[Map showing two fields comparison labelled 1950 (top) with field A in centre, and 2000 (bottom). Key: Farm (square), Farm boundary. Fields: Wheat (vertical lines), Barley (horizontal lines), Potatoes (dots).]

(a) Complete **Figure 1** to show that field A was used for growing wheat in 1950.
(1 mark)

(b) (i) Using the information shown in **Figure 1**, describe how farming has changed between 1950 and 2000.

Look for changes in the size of farms and the type of crops grown.

....
....
....
....
(3 marks)

(ii) Explain how these changes could have a negative impact on the environment.

....
....
....
....
(2 marks)

(iii) Describe one other way modern farming practices negatively affect the environment.

....
(1 mark)

2   Study **Figure 2**, an extract from an article about a farm.

(a) What is the name of the type of farming carried out on Hilltop Farm?

....
(1 mark)

Figure 2

> No artificial pesticides or fertilisers are used on Hilltop Farm, and despite producing lower yields than its neighbours, Hilltop continues to make a good profit. This is partly due to increased demand for its produce, and partly thanks to government policies that encourage environmentally-friendly farming.

(b) Using information from **Figure 2** and your own knowledge, give two reasons why demand for produce from this type of farm is increasing.

....
....
....
(2 marks)

(c) Describe a government policy that aims to reduce the environmental impact of farming.

....
....
(2 marks)

Unit 2A — Changing Rural Environments

Change in UK Commercial Farming

3 Study **Figure 3**, which shows how the quantity and source of food consumed in Byrnshire has changed between 1960 and 2000.

Figure 3

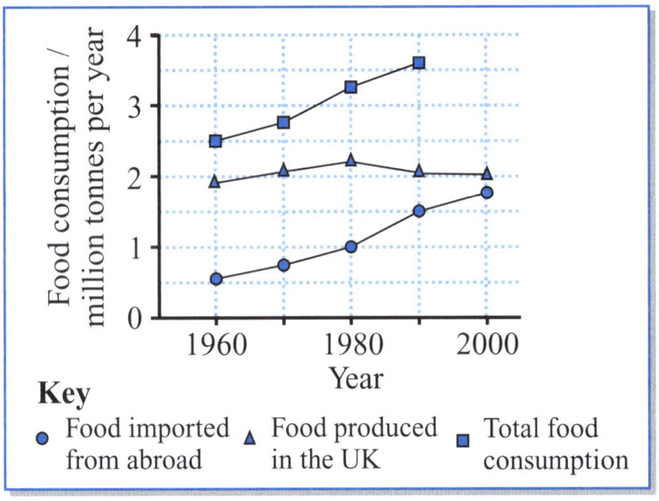

[Graph showing Food consumption / million tonnes per year on y-axis (0 to 4) against Year on x-axis (1960 to 2000). Key: Food imported from abroad (circles), Food produced in the UK (triangles), Total food consumption (squares).]

(a) Complete **Figure 3** to show that 3.75 million tonnes of food was consumed in Byrnshire in 2000.
(1 mark)

(b) Calculate the percentage of the total food consumed in Byrnshire in 2000 that was produced in the UK.

....
....
(1 mark)

(c) Use **Figure 3** to describe how the nature of food consumption in Byrnshire has changed.

....
....
....
....

Comment on all the trends shown in the graph.

(3 marks)

(d) Suggest how the changes shown by **Figure 3** have benefited consumers in Byrnshire.

....
(1 mark)

(e) Explain the effect that the change in the amount of imported food might have on UK farmers.

....
....
....
(3 marks)

(f) 69% of all food in Byrnshire is purchased from supermarkets.
Explain why this forces farmers to keep their prices low.

....
....
(1 mark)

4 Describe how farming practices have changed in one commercial farming area in the UK that you have studied.

(8 marks)
spelling, punctuation and grammar: 3 marks

Unit 2A — Changing Rural Environments

Sustainable Rural Living

1 Study **Figure 1**, which is an extract from an article about Community Rail Partnerships.

(a) What does the term 'sustainable living' mean?

....

....

....

....
(2 marks)

Figure 1

Local Railway Cash Success
 The Ecklethwaite - Nabstable Support Group is celebrating today after receiving a grant of £5000 from the government-run Community Rail Partnership. The money is to be spent on improved cycle storage facilities at Ecklethwaite station, and a shelter for rail and connecting bus passengers.
 A spokesman said "Community Rail Partnerships aim to increase local train use by improving bus links, cycle routes and station buildings, to promote more sustainable living in rural areas".

(b) Explain how Community Rail Partnerships help towards more sustainable living in rural areas.

....

....

....

....

....

....
(6 marks)

(c) Describe one other government initiative that protects the rural economy and environment.

....

....

....

....
(4 marks)

Don't waste time describing more than one initiative.

2 Study **Figure 2**, which shows potato yields for fields with different amounts of irrigation.

Figure 2

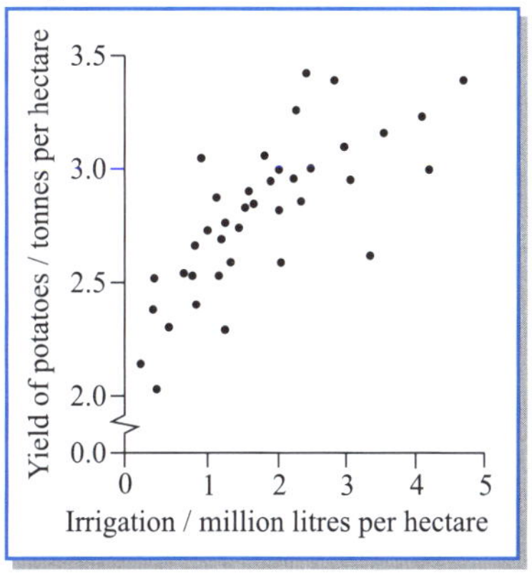

(Scatter graph: Yield of potatoes / tonnes per hectare vs Irrigation / million litres per hectare)

(a) What type of correlation does **Figure 2** show?

....
(1 mark)

(b) Suggest why irrigation is sometimes unsustainable.

....
(1 mark)

(c) Suggest two ways, other than by reducing irrigation, that farming can be done more sustainably.

....

....
(2 marks)

Unit 2A — Changing Rural Environments

Changes to Farming in Tropical Areas

1   Study **Figure 1** which shows the changing nature of farming in Lartua between 1960 and 2000. Lartua is a poor rural area in the tropics.

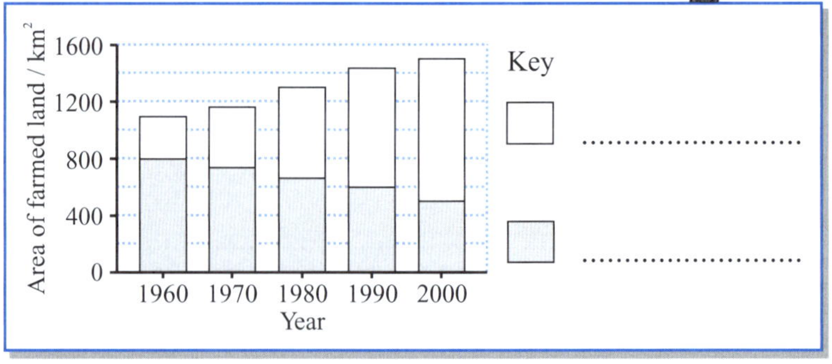

   (a) (i) Complete the key for **Figure 1** by adding 'subsistence farming' and 'commercial farming' in the correct places.
   (1 mark)

   Figure 1

   (ii) What is commercial farming?

   ....
   (1 mark)

   (iii) How much land was used for commercial farming in Lartua in 2000?..................................
   (1 mark)

   (b) (i) Using the information in **Figure 1**, describe how the nature of farming in Lartua changed between 1960 and 2000. ....

   ....

   ....

   ....
   (3 marks)

   (ii) Suggest two impacts of the change to commercial farming in the area.

   ....

   ....
   (2 marks)

2   Study **Figure 2**, which gives information about an appropriate technology used in Lesotho, a small country in southern Africa.

   Figure 2

   > Farmers in Lesotho have benefited from drip irrigation, which uses a network of pipes to slowly supply water from a tank directly to the roots of plants. This simple, low cost technology means much less water is wasted, and allows people to grow fruit and vegetables for their household even during the dry season.

   (a) Explain why the technique outlined in **Figure 2** can be described as an appropriate technology.

   ....
   (1 mark)

   (b) Describe another example of an appropriate technology that has been used to increase food production.

   ....

   ....

   ....
   (3 marks)

Unit 2A — Changing Rural Environments

Changes to Farming in Tropical Areas

3   Study **Figure 3**, which shows how irrigation levels have changed in Bangolo, a rural region located in a tropical climate.

Figure 3

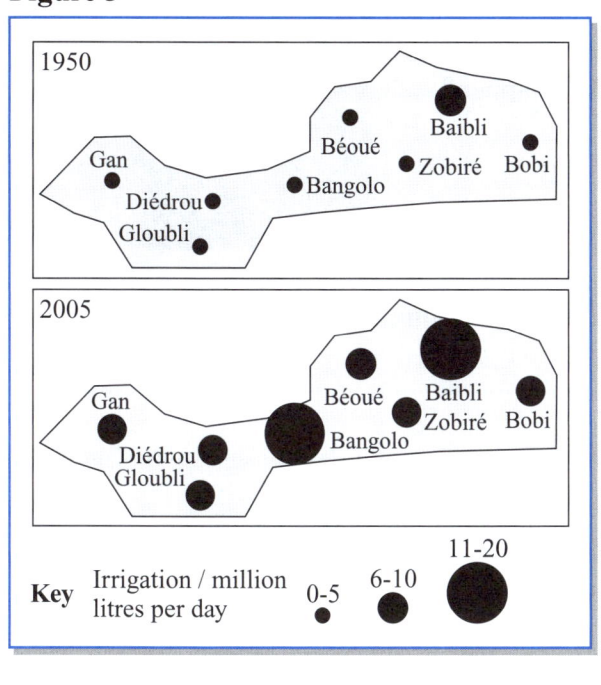

(1950 and 2005 maps of Bangolo region showing irrigation levels at Gan, Diédrou, Gloubli, Béoué, Bangolo, Baibli, Zobiré, Bobi)

Key Irrigation / million litres per day   0-5   6-10   11-20

(a) (i) How much water was used for irrigation in Gan in 2005?

....
(1 mark)

(ii) Irrigation increased in all areas between 1950 and 2005. Give a reason, other than a decrease in rainfall, that could have caused this trend.

....
....
....
(1 mark)

(b) Describe the impacts that irrigation can have on the environment.

The question doesn't specify what type of impact, so you need to include positive and negative ones.

....
....
....
....
....
....
(6 marks)

(c) How might irrigation have improved people's lives in Bangolo?

....
....
(2 marks)

(d) Increased irrigation can increase the percentage of people infected with malaria, due to mosquitoes breeding in irrigation ditches. Study **Figure 4**, which shows the percentage of people in Bangolo that were infected in 1950 and in 2005. What was the percentage difference between those infected in 1950 and 2005?

Figure 4

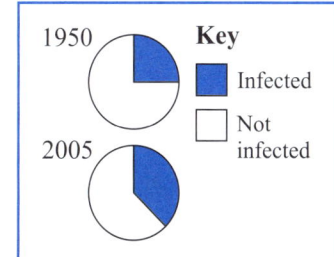

(Pie charts for 1950 and 2005 with Key: Infected / Not infected)

....
(1 mark)

Unit 2A — Changing Rural Environments

Factors Affecting Farming in Tropical Areas

1   Study **Figure 1**, which shows an area of agricultural land in a tropical region.

   (a) (i) Name the process that is occurring in **Figure 1**.

   ....
   (1 mark)

   Figure 1

   (ii) How can overgrazing cause this process to happen?

   ....
   ....
   (1 mark)

   (b) Explain the impacts this process could have on a rural community.

   ....
   ....

   To answer this question you need to describe the impacts and say how the process leads to them.

   ....
   (3 marks)

2   Study **Figure 2**, which shows land use and migration of people in the tropical Kolurna region.

   (a) Name the type of migration shown in **Figure 2**.

   ....
   (1 mark)

   Figure 2

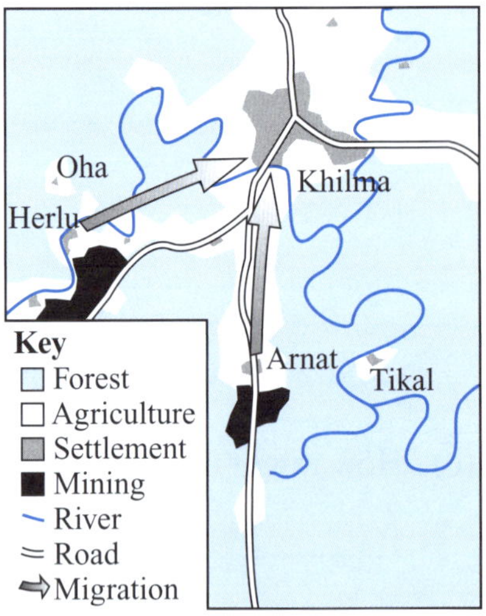

   (b) (i) Many people are migrating from Herlu due to the impact of nearby mining. Describe one way mining can affect subsistence farming.

   ....
   ....
   ....
   (1 mark)

   Key
   ☐ Forest
   ☐ Agriculture
   ▨ Settlement
   ■ Mining
   ～ River
   ═ Road
   ⇨ Migration

   (ii) Name another human activity that affects subsistence farming and explain one way that it affects it.

   ....
   ....
   ....
   (2 marks)

   (c) Describe one impact that the migration shown in **Figure 1** might have on the city of Khilma.

   ....
   (1 mark)

Unit 2A — Changing Rural Environments

Unit 2B — The Development Gap

Measuring Development

1. Study **Figure 1**, which shows measures of development for Canada, Taiwan and Angola.

   Figure 1

	Canada	Taiwan	Angola
GNI per capita*	$32 220	$22 900	$2210
Birth rate	10.3	9.0	43.7
Death rate	7.7	6.8	24.1
Infant mortality rate	5.0	5.4	180.2
Life expectancy	81.2	78.0	38.2
Literacy rate	99.0%	96.1%	67.4%

   * GNI per capita information from Hutchinson Country Facts. © RM, 2009. All rights reserved. Helicon Publishing is a division of RM.

   (a) (i) What is meant by the Gross National Income (GNI) per capita of a country?

   ....
   ....
   ....
   (2 marks)

   (ii) Define birth rate.

   ....
   (1 mark)

   (iii) Using **Figure 1**, explain which country is the most developed.

   Try to include all the measures mentioned in Figure 1 in your answer.

   ....
   ....
   ....
   (3 marks)

   (iv) Explain the correlation between GNI per capita and literacy rate shown in **Figure 1**.

   ....
   ....
   (2 marks)

(b) Give two limitations of using a single measure of development to judge how developed a country is.

   Limitation 1 ....
   ....
   Limitation 2 ....
   ....
   (2 marks)

(c) Explain why the HDI is a useful measure of development.

   Make sure you say what HDI is before you say why it's useful.

   ....
   ....
   ....
   (2 marks)

Global Inequalities

1   Study **Figure 1**, which shows the global distribution of MEDCs and LEDCs.

Figure 1

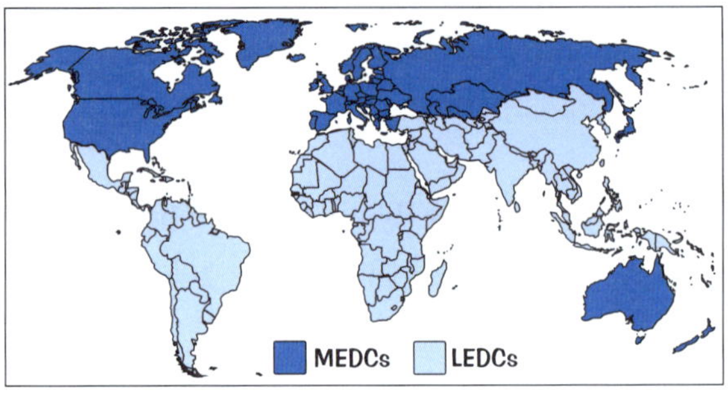

(MEDCs / LEDCs world map)

(a) Describe the global distribution of MEDCs and LEDCs.

....

....

....

....

(3 marks)

(b) Give one problem with classifying countries as MEDCs or LEDCs.

....

(1 mark)

(c) Describe a more acceptable classification system.

....

....

....

....

....

Decide what you want to say before you start writing your answer — that way it will flow better and you won't miss anything out.

(6 marks)

Figure 2

	UK	Mozambique
PQLI	99.9	28.4
Number of mobile phones per 1000 people	1236.5	203.3

2   Study **Figure 2**, which shows the PQLI (Physical Quality of Life Index, an indicator of quality of life) and the number of mobile phones per 1000 people (an indicator of standard of living) in two countries.

(a) Using **Figure 2**, compare quality of life and standard of living in the UK and Mozambique.

....

....

....

(2 marks)

(b) Explain the difference between standard of living and quality of life.

....

Include examples in your answer to back up your points.

....

(2 marks)

Unit 2B — The Development Gap

Causes of Global Inequalities

1   Study **Figure 1**, which shows the percentage of people with access to clean water and the HDI values of four countries in 2006-2007.

Figure 1

	% of population with access to clean water	HDI
Chad	48	0.389
Ethiopia	42	0.389
Uganda	64	0.493
Pakistan	90	0.562

(a) Compare the percentage of the population who have access to clean water in Pakistan and Ethiopia.

....

....

(1 mark)

(b) Describe and explain the correlation between the availability of clean water in a country and its level of development (shown by its HDI value).

Don't forget to 'describe' AND 'explain'.

....

....

....

....

....

(4 marks)

2   **Figure 2**

[Scatter graph: HDI (y-axis, 0 to 1.0) vs Literacy rate / % (x-axis, 0 to 100). Points approximately at (20, 0.38), (55, 0.55), (80, 0.7), (80, 0.85), (90, 0.9), (95, 0.9).]

Study **Figure 2**, which is a scatter graph showing the HDI value and literacy rate for six countries in 2006.

(a) Describe the correlation between literacy rate and development.

....

....

(1 mark)

(b) The literacy rate in Mali in 2006 was 22.9. What was its HDI score?

....

(1 mark)

(c) Suggest why a low literacy rate could have a negative impact on development.

....

....

....

(3 marks)

Unit 2B — The Development Gap

Causes of Global Inequalities

3 Tsunamis are natural hazards that can affect a country's development. Study **Figure 3**, a photograph taken in Indonesia after a tsunami.

(a) (i) Give one impact of the tsunami that can be seen in **Figure 3**.

....
(1 mark)

(ii) What is meant by the term 'natural hazard'?

....
....
(1 mark)

Figure 3

©iStockphoto.com/Justin Long

(b) For an area you have studied, describe and explain how a natural disaster has affected its development.
(8 marks)
spelling, punctuation and grammar: 3 marks

4 In 2007, Nicaragua had a 0.01% share of the world's total exports while the UK had a 3.04% share. Study **Figure 4**, which shows the types of goods exported by each country.

Figure 4

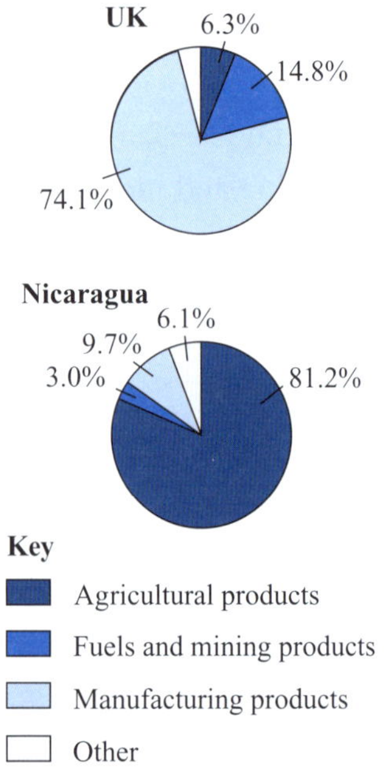

UK
6.3%
14.8%
74.1%

Nicaragua
6.1%
9.7%
3.0%
81.2%

Key
- Agricultural products
- Fuels and mining products
- Manufacturing products
- Other

(a) (i) In 2007, Nicaragua generated US$1225 million from exports. Using **Figure 4**, calculate how much money was generated from the export of fuels and mining products.

....
(1 mark)

(ii) In 2007, what percentage of UK exports was not agricultural products, fuels or mining products?

Include your working for any calculations.

....
(1 mark)

(iii) Using **Figure 4**, explain why Nicaragua is less developed than the UK.

....
....
....
....
(2 marks)

(b) Explain how poor trade links affect a country's development.

....
....
(2 marks)

Unit 2B — The Development Gap

Causes of Global Inequalities

5   Study **Figure 5**, which shows the change in HDI for three countries between 1990 and 2005.

Figure 5

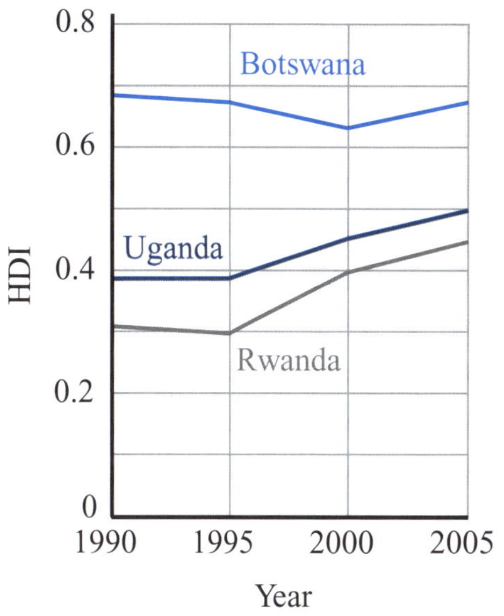

(a) (i) What was the HDI for Rwanda in 1995?

....
(1 mark)

(ii) Describe how the HDI for Botswana changed between 1990 and 2005.

Make sure you refer to the figure in your answer — mention specific HDI values for different years.

....
....
....
....
(2 marks)

(iii) The government of Uganda has been accused of corruption. Describe and explain how a corrupt or unstable government can affect a country's development.

....
....
....
....
(4 marks)

(b) Egypt's HDI increased steadily from 0.58 to 0.70 between 1990 and 2005.

(i) Using evidence from **Figure 5**, compare the HDI of Uganda and Egypt.

....
....
(2 marks)

(ii) Egypt has very low rainfall. Suggest how this may have limited Egypt's development.

....
....
....
....
(4 marks)

Unit 2B — The Development Gap

Reducing Global Inequality

1 Study **Figure 1**, a newspaper article about a self-help scheme in Kenya.

Figure 1

Self-help in Kenya's slums

The Kibera Youth Self-Help Group (KYSG) is on a mission to clear up the Kianda village area of the Kibera slums. Originally founded by three men in 2001, the group has grown to work with around 200 children including orphans, street kids and jobless youths.

One of the first things the group did was to clear up the community dumping area. They started a solid waste collection scheme and disposed of the waste responsibly in designated areas. They've followed it up with a recycling scheme to collect and sell plastic waste. The group's offices are based on the old dumping ground, which now also boasts car washing bays and carpet cleaning facilities.

(a) Suggest how KYSG's activities can improve quality of life for the whole Kibera community.

....

....

....

....

(4 marks)

(b) Suggest two other ways people in poor areas try to improve their own quality of life.

....

....

(2 marks)

2 Study **Figure 2**, which shows the annual income of a farmer in Mali between 1994 and 2002. He joined a fair trade co-operative in 1996.

Figure 2

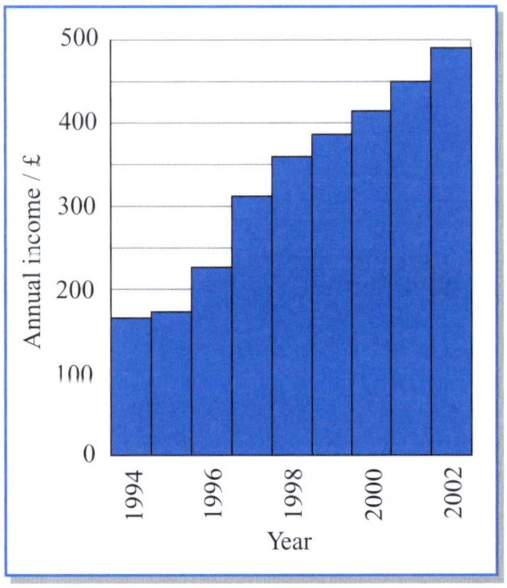

(a) What was the farmer's income in 1999?

....

(1 mark)

(b) Using evidence from **Figure 2**, explain how fair trade schemes can affect a country's development.

....

....

....

....

....

(4 marks)

Unit 2B — The Development Gap

Reducing Global Inequality

3 The North American Free Trade Agreement (NAFTA) is a trading group made up of the USA, Canada and Mexico. It took effect in 1994 and aims to eliminate trade barriers between them. Study **Figure 3**, which shows the value of exports and imports between the NAFTA countries in 1993 and 2008.

Figure 3

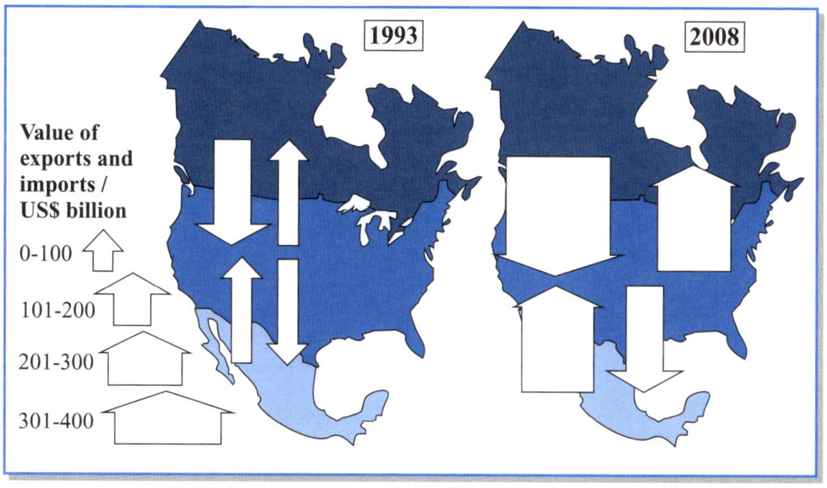

(a) (i) What was the value of USA exports to Mexico in 2008?

Make sure you read the key carefully and get the units right.

....
....
(1 mark)

(ii) How did the value of USA exports to Canada change between 1993 and 2008?

....
(1 mark)

(iii) With reference to **Figure 3**, suggest how joining NAFTA may have affected Mexico's development. Explain your answer.

....
....
....
(4 marks)

(b) Describe how trading groups can cause problems for poorer non-member countries.

....
....
(2 marks)

4 Bolivia was one of the first countries to make a conservation swap agreement. The agreement with Conservation International in 1987 led to the cancellation of $650 000 of debt.

(a) What is a conservation swap?

....
(1 mark)

(b) Suggest how the conservation swap agreement could have affected Bolivia's development.

....
....
(2 marks)

Unit 2B — The Development Gap

Reducing Global Inequality

5   Study **Figure 4**, a newspaper article about an aid project in Ghana.

Figure 4

> ### UK Government Support for Ghana
>
> The UK is the second largest aid donor to Ghana. The UK Government's Department for International Development (DFID) gave over £205 million between 2005 and 2007 towards Ghana's poverty reduction plans. This level of aid continues, with donations of around £85 million per year. The aid is used in several ways, including to improve healthcare, education and sanitation.
>
> About 15% of the UK's funding in 2008 was used to support the healthcare system in Ghana — £42.5 million was pledged to support the Ghanaian Government's 2008-2012 health plan. On top of that, in 2008 the UK gave nearly £7 million to buy emergency equipment to reduce maternal deaths.
>
> Thanks to a £105 million grant from the UK in 2006, Ghana has been able to set up a ten year education strategic plan. It was the first African country to do this. The UK pledged additional money to help 12 000 children in North Ghana to get a formal basic education.

(a) (i) Is the aid described in **Figure 4** an example of multilateral aid or bilateral aid?

....

(1 mark)

(ii) Suggest the potential advantages and disadvantages for the recipient country of long-term aid projects such as the one described in **Figure 4**.

....

This is a 4 mark question, so try to come up with two advantages and two disadvantages.

....

....

....

(4 marks)

(b) Describe what is meant by sustainable aid and explain whether the aid described in **Figure 4** is sustainable.

....

....

....

(3 marks)

(c) What is meant by 'short-term aid'?

....

(1 mark)

(d) Give one disadvantage of aid projects for the donor country.

....

(1 mark)

(e) Explain how a development project you have studied is benefiting the recipient country.

(8 marks)
spelling, punctuation and grammar: 3 marks

Unit 2B — The Development Gap

Inequalities in the EU

1   The European Union's Regional Development Fund (ERDF) invests money in sustainable development projects in urban areas. Study **Figure 1**, which shows the locations of URBAN Community Initiative development projects in the UK that received a contribution from the ERDF programmes of 1994-1999 and 2000-2006.

Figure 1

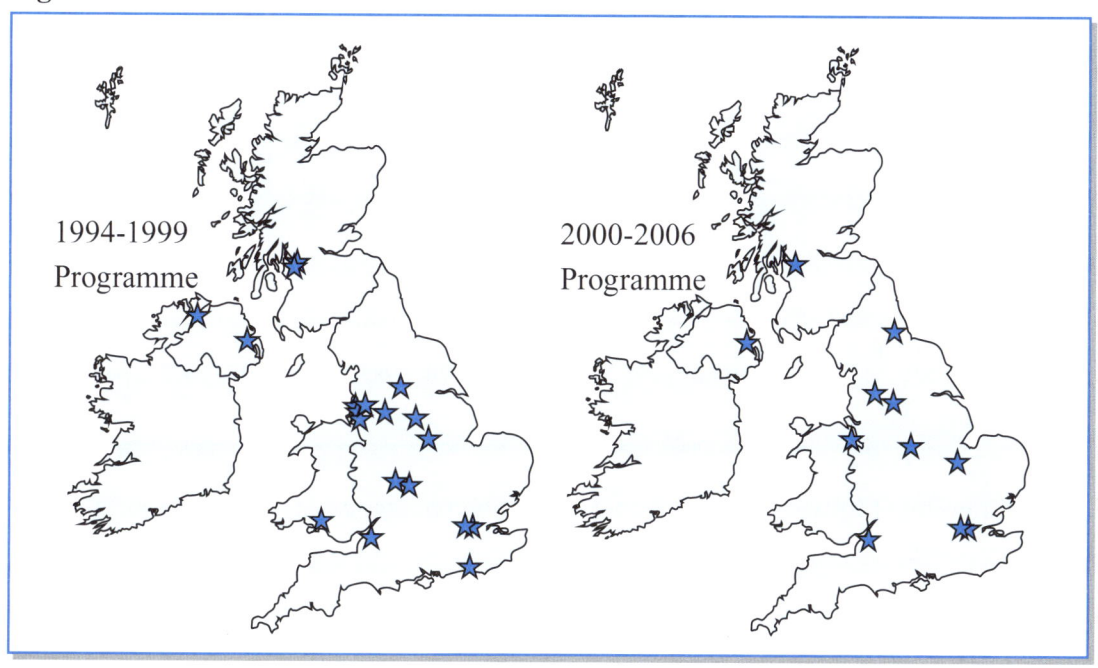

1994-1999 Programme

2000-2006 Programme

(a) (i)   Using **Figure 1**, describe the distribution of urban development projects in the UK in the 1994-1999 programme.

....

....
(2 marks)

(ii)   How did the distribution of urban development projects change for the 2000-2006 programme?

....

....
(2 marks)

(b)   Other than the ERDF, describe one way in which the EU has tried to reduce inequalities across its member countries.

....

....

....
(3 marks)

(c)   Describe and explain the development levels of two contrasting EU countries you have studied.
(8 marks)
spelling, punctuation and grammar: 3 marks

Unit 2B — The Development Gap

Unit 2B — Globalisation

Globalisation Basics

1   Improvements in air transport are partly responsible for the increase in globalisation.
    Study **Figure 1**, which shows the number of passengers using UK airports from 1950 to 2000.

Figure 1

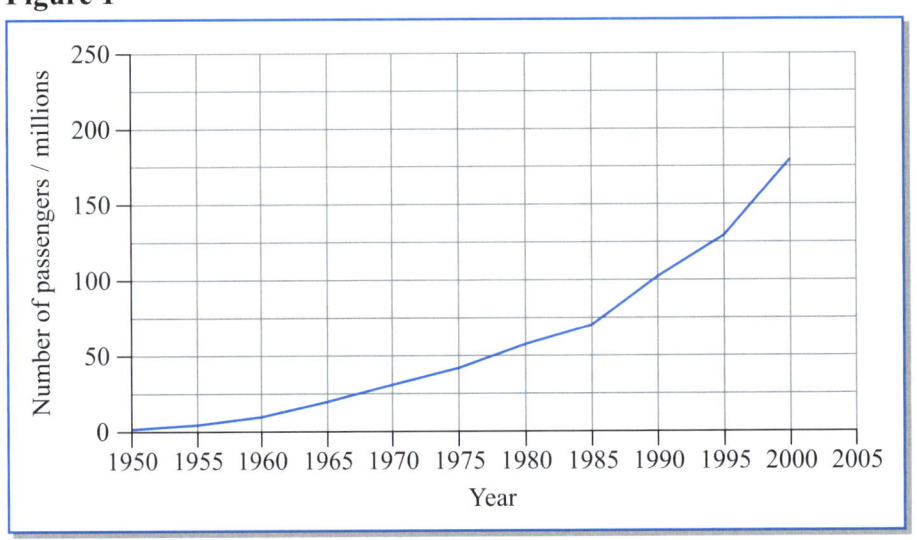

[Line graph: x-axis "Year" from 1950 to 2005; y-axis "Number of passengers / millions" from 0 to 250. Curve rises slowly from near 0 in 1950 to about 10 in 1960, ~30 in 1970, ~60 in 1980, ~70 in 1985, ~110 in 1990, ~130 in 1995, ~180 in 2000.]

(a) (i)   Complete **Figure 1** to show that 228 million passengers used UK airports in 2005.
(1 mark)

   (ii) Using **Figure 1**, calculate the difference between the number
         of passengers using UK airports in 1960 and in 2000.
   ....
(1 mark)

(b) (i)   What is meant by the term 'globalisation'?
   ....
(1 mark)

   (ii) Explain how improvements in air transport have increased globalisation.
   ....
   ....
(2 marks)

   (iii) Globalisation has caused countries to become interdependent.
         Explain what interdependent means.
   ....
(1 mark)

(c) Explain why some companies have moved their call centres abroad.
   ....
   ....
   ....
(3 marks)

In the exam you get roughly one minute per mark to answer, so spend about three minutes on this answer.

Trans-National Corporations (TNCs)

1   Study **Figure 1**, which shows the distribution of Mega Lomania (a TNC) around the world.

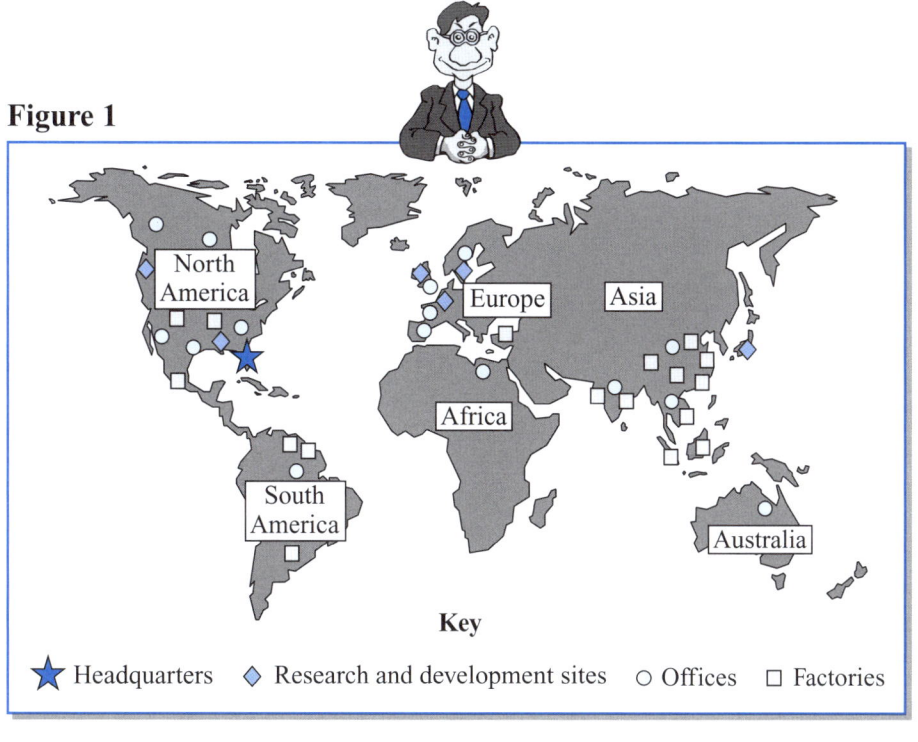

Figure 1

Key
★ Headquarters   ◆ Research and development sites   ○ Offices   □ Factories

(a) What is meant by the term 'Trans-National Corporation' (TNC)?

....
(1 mark)

(b) Use **Figure 1** to describe and explain the distribution of Mega Lomania's sites.

....

....

Talk about general patterns when you're describing a distribution.

....

(4 marks)

(c) Give two advantages of TNCs locating in places like south east Asia.

....

....
(2 marks)

(d) How do TNCs like Mega Lomania increase globalisation?

....
(1 mark)

2   For a named TNC that you have studied, describe the advantages
    and disadvantages it has brought to different countries.

(8 marks)
spelling, punctuation and grammar: 3 marks

Unit 2B — Globalisation

Change in Manufacturing Location

1   Mega Lomania has moved all of its factories from Ingerland (a rich country) to Bonechina (a Newly Industrialising Country). Study **Figure 1**, which compares working conditions in the two countries.

(a) (i) Using **Figure 1**, calculate the difference between the maximum wage per week for a factory worker in Ingerland and Bonechina.

Figure 1

	Ingerland	Bonechina
Minimum wage / hour	£6.12	£0.63
Maximum number of working hours per week	40	80
Health and safety	Very strict	Very lax

....

....
(2 marks)

(ii) Use **Figure 1** to suggest why Mega Lomania has moved its factories to Bonechina.

....

....

....

....

....

....

....
(6 marks)

(iii) Describe one other reason why factories are moved to Newly Industrialising Countries.

....

....
(2 marks)

(b) Many other TNCs are moving their factories out of Ingerland to countries like Bonechina. This is leading to deindustrialisation.

Make sure you know the definitions of tricky geographical words.

(i) Describe what is meant by 'deindustrialisation'.

....
(1 mark)

(ii) Describe the effects of deindustrialisation on countries like Ingerland.

....

....
(2 marks)

2   Describe and explain the recent growth in manufacturing in China.
(8 marks)
spelling, punctuation and grammar: 3 marks

Unit 2B — Globalisation

Globalisation and Energy Demand

1   Study **Figure 1**, which shows the world's actual and predicted energy consumption.

(a) Complete **Figure 1** to show that the world's predicted energy consumption in 2025 will be 640 quadrillion Btu.
(1 mark)

Figure 1

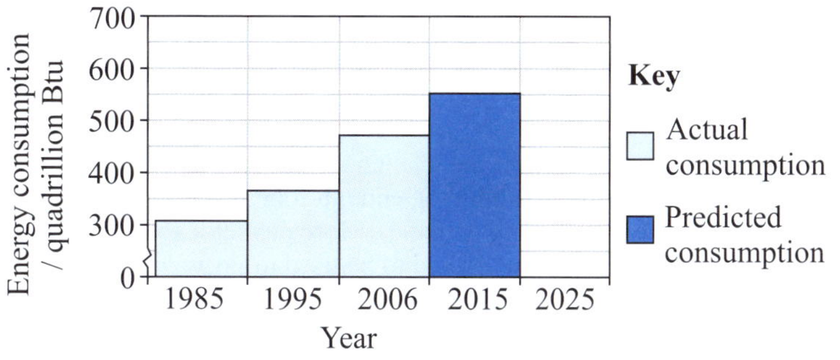

(b) (i) Explain why globalisation has increased the global demand for energy.

....
....
(2 marks)

(ii) Give one other reason why the global demand for energy is increasing.

....
(1 mark)

Figure 2

Key
• Potential nuclear power plant site

(c) Study **Figure 2**, which shows the potential sites for new nuclear power plants in the UK.

(i) Describe the distribution of the sites around the UK.

....
....
(2 marks)

(ii) Explain one social impact of building more nuclear power plants.

....
....
....
(2 marks)

Remember, impacts don't have to be negative.

(d) Describe and explain the environmental impacts of producing more energy from fossil fuels.

....
....
....
....
....
(6 marks)

Unit 2B — Globalisation

Globalisation and Food Supply

1 Study **Figure 1**, which is an article about the increase in global food demand.

Figure 1

> **GLOBAL FOOD DEMAND GROWING OUT OF CONTROL**
>
> Over the last 40 years there has been a large increase in the amount of food consumed globally. One of the challenges in years to come will be producing enough food to meet the ever-growing demand. More pesticides and fertilisers will need to be used to grow food in massive quantities. Producing more food will also increase the demand on water supplies — between 1980 and 2002 the area of irrigated land in the world increased by over 600 000 km², and this will keep growing. Many countries are importing food from around the world to meet their demands, which has caused an increase in commercial farming of cash crops in places like Brazil, Thailand and Africa.

(a) Suggest a reason for the increased global demand for food.

....

(1 mark)

(b) (i) Describe how commercial farming is different from subsistence farming.

....

(1 mark)

(ii) Explain the problems caused by switching from subsistence to commercial farming.

....

....

....

(2 marks)

(c) (i) What term is given to the distance food is transported to its market?

....

(1 mark)

(ii) Describe one negative impact of importing food from around the world.

....

....

(2 marks)

(d) Use **Figure 1** to explain the other impacts of meeting the demand for more food, besides an increase in commercial farming and the increase in food imports.

....

....

....

....

(4 marks)

Unit 2B — Globalisation

Reducing the Impacts of Globalisation

1   Study **Figure 1**, which shows the electricity production from renewable sources in an area.

Figure 1

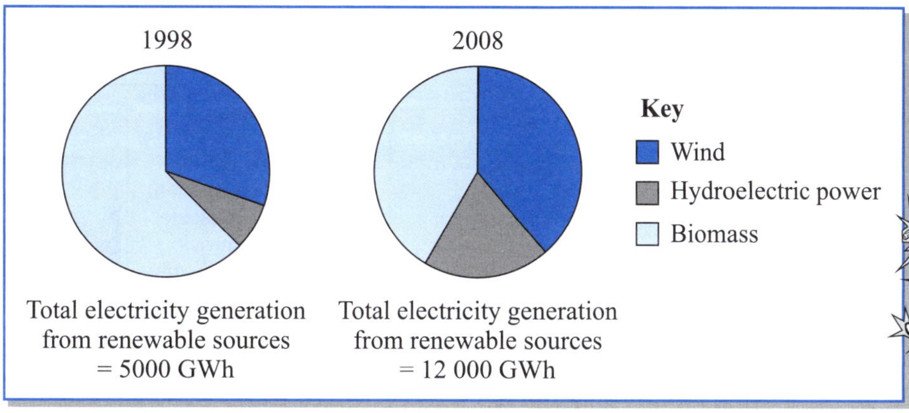

1998 | 2008

Key
- Wind
- Hydroelectric power
- Biomass

Total electricity generation from renewable sources = 5000 GWh

Total electricity generation from renewable sources = 12 000 GWh

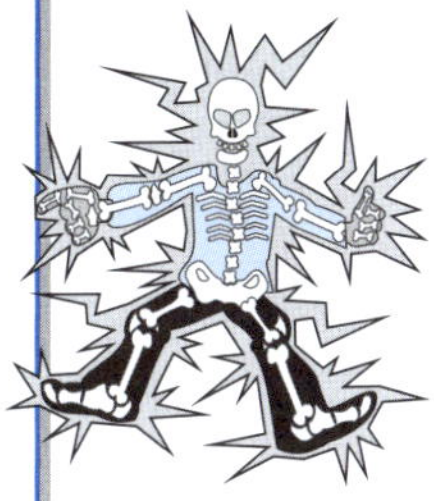

(a) (i)   Using **Figure 1**, calculate the amount of electricity produced using biomass in 2008.

....
(1 mark)

(ii)   Calculate the difference in the amount of electricity produced using wind between 1998 and 2008.

Don't forget to put the units at the end of your answer.

....

....
(3 marks)

(b) (i)   Describe how electricity can be generated using hydroelectric power.

....

....
(2 marks)

(ii)   Describe another renewable energy source that isn't mentioned in **Figure 1**.

....

....
(2 marks)

(c)   Contrast the sustainability of renewable and non-renewable energy sources.

....

Contrast means write about the differences.

....

....
(3 marks)

2   Describe a renewable energy source that you have studied and the impacts it has had.

(8 marks)
spelling, punctuation and grammar: 3 marks

Unit 2B — Globalisation

Reducing the Impacts of Globalisation

3   Study **Figure 2**, which is an extract from an article on the Kyoto Protocol.

(a) Use **Figure 2** to explain why countries want to reduce carbon dioxide emissions.

....

....

....

....
(2 marks)

Figure 2

THE KYOTO PROTOCOL

Global warming is causing sea level to rise and extreme weather events to happen more frequently. To tackle the issue, countries have signed the Kyoto Protocol. They have to monitor and cut emissions of carbon dioxide and other gases by 2012. Each country has agreed to reach an emissions target and the carbon credits trading scheme encourages them to meet their targets.

(b) Describe how the carbon credits scheme works to help reduce carbon dioxide emissions.

....

....

The number of marks gives you an idea of the level of detail that's needed.

....

....
(4 marks)

4   Study **Figure 3**, which shows the average level of ozone (a pollutant at low altitude) in urban areas in the UK.

(a) Complete **Figure 3** to show that the level of ozone in 2004 was 57 micrograms per cubic metre.
(1 mark)

Figure 3

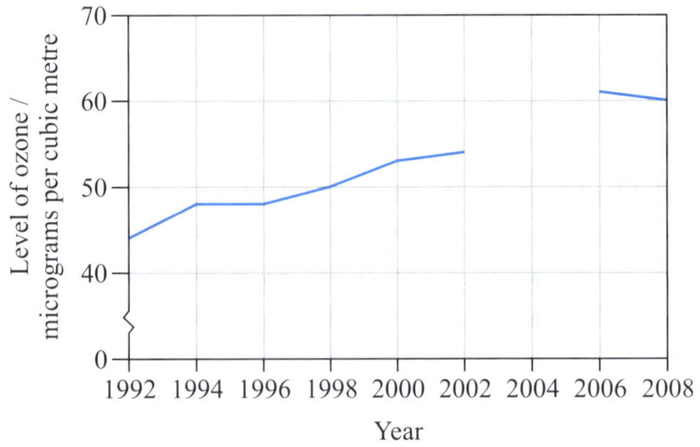

(b) Using **Figure 3**, describe the change in the level of ozone between 1992 and 2008.

....

....
(2 marks)

(c) Describe an international agreement to control pollution, apart from the Kyoto Protocol.

....

....
(2 marks)

Unit 2B — Globalisation

Reducing the Impacts of Globalisation

5   Study **Figure 4**, which shows waste disposal methods in the different districts of a county.

Figure 4

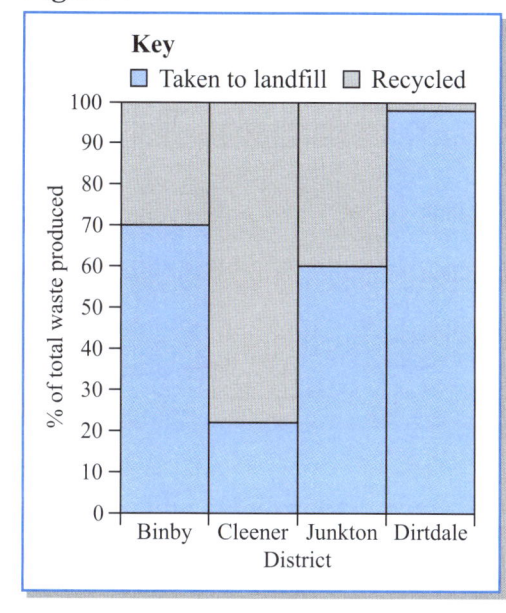

(a) (i) What percentage of the waste produced in Cleener was recycled?

....
(1 mark)

(ii) The waste produced in Dirtdale weighed a total of 400 000 tonnes. Calculate the weight of Dirtdale's waste that was taken to landfill.

....

....
(2 marks)

(b) Explain the impact of increased globalisation on waste production and how recycling reduces the impact.

....

....

....
(3 marks)

6   Study **Figure 5**, which shows the average amount spent per month on local produce in a town.

Figure 5

Year	1989	1994	1999	2004	2009
Amount	£8.22	£9.50	£10.80	£12.68	£16.70

(a) Using **Figure 5**, describe the change in the amount spent on local produce from 1989 to 2009.

'Using figure' means using numbers or facts from the figure in your answer.

....

....
(2 marks)

(b) Describe the advantages and disadvantages of buying local produce.

....

....

....
(3 marks)

Unit 2B — Globalisation

Unit 2B — Tourism

Growth in Tourism

1. Study **Figure 1**, which shows the most popular tourist destinations in Bremma.

   Figure 1

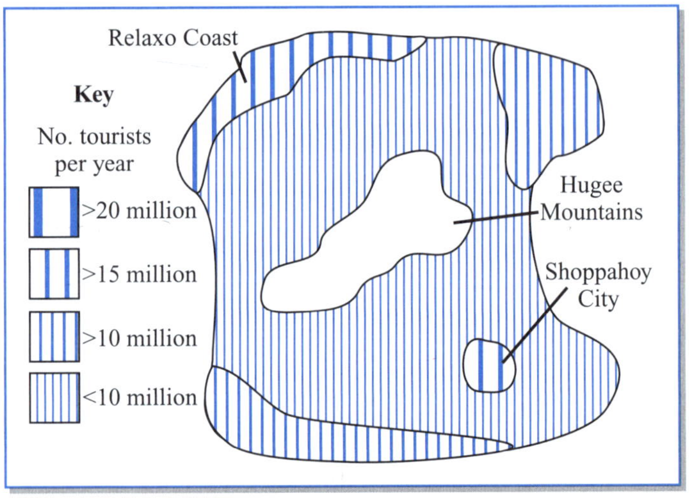

   (Key: No. tourists per year: >20 million, >15 million, >10 million, <10 million. Labels: Relaxo Coast, Hugee Mountains, Shoppahoy City)

   (a) (i) Complete **Figure 1** to show that 22 million tourists visit the Hugee Mountains each year.
   (1 mark)

   (ii) Suggest why the three most visited areas in **Figure 1** are the most popular with tourists.

   ....
   ....
   ....
   ....
   (3 marks)

   (b) Study **Figure 2**, which shows the number of visits abroad made by UK residents between 1999 and 2006.
   Suggest reasons for the trend shown in **Figure 2**.

   Figure 2
   (Line graph: No. of visits abroad / millions vs Year 1999–2006, rising from ~54 to ~70)

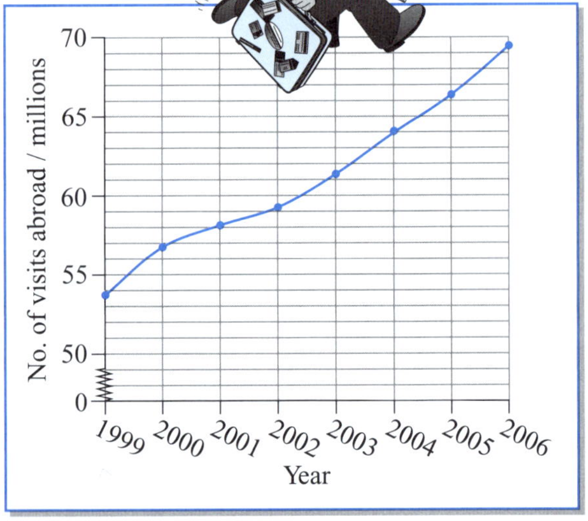

   ....
   ....
   ....
   ....
   ....
   ....
   (4 marks)

   (c) (i) Give two reasons why tourism is an important economic activity.

   ....
   ....
   (2 marks)

   (ii) Contrast the economic importance of tourism in rich and poor countries.

   'Contrast' means write about the differences.

   ....
   ....
   (2 marks)

UK Tourism

1 Study **Figure 1**, an extract from a report into tourism in the UK.

Figure 1

A thriving tourist industry is important for a healthy economy. Data collected over a ten year period shows that the UK continues to be a popular tourist destination, with London being a major attraction for overseas tourists.
Many experts suggest the recent trend in numbers reflects the worldwide recession. The UK tourist industry can look forward to brighter times ahead though, as the 2012 Olympic Games (to be held in London) are expected to attract up to 6.6 million extra visitors to the city.

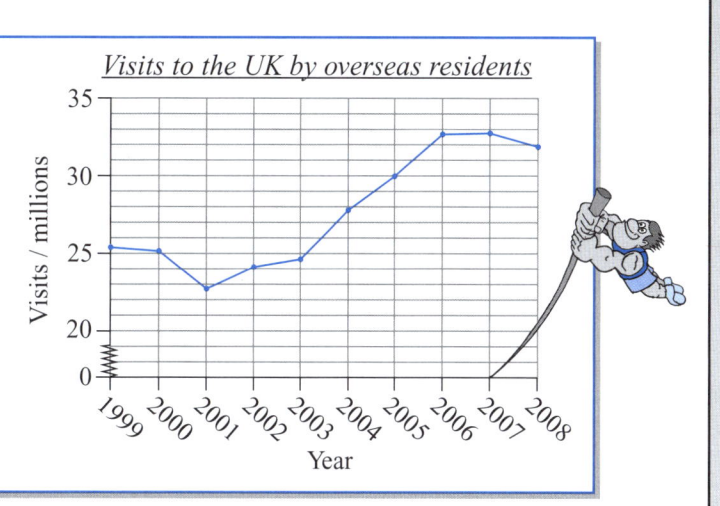

Visits to the UK by overseas residents

(a) (i) How many visits to the UK from overseas were there in 2005?

....

(1 mark)

(ii) Use **Figure 1** to describe how the number of tourists visiting the UK has changed between 1999 and 2008.

....

....

(2 marks)

(b) (i) Give a reason why huge numbers of tourists are attracted to London each year.

....

(1 mark)

(ii) Explain the importance of major events such as the Olympic Games to the UK's economy.

....

....

....

(3 marks)

(c) Describe three factors, other than major events such as the Olympic Games, that can affect visitor numbers to the UK.

Numbers can go up or down, so the factors can be positive or negative.

....

....

....

....

(3 marks)

Unit 2B — Tourism

UK Tourism

2   Study **Figure 2**, which shows the life cycle of a coastal tourist resort.

Figure 2

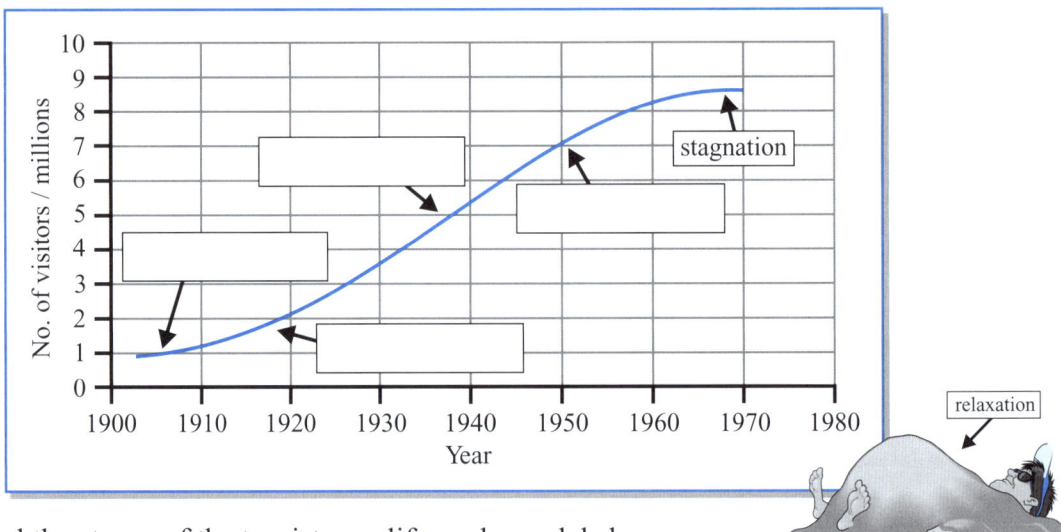

[Graph showing number of visitors (millions) vs Year from 1900 to 1980, with an S-shaped curve rising from ~1 million in 1900 to ~8.5 million by 1970. Labels point to different stages of the curve, with "stagnation" labelled near the top and "relaxation" labelled to the side.]

(a) (i)   Label the stages of the tourist area life cycle model shown in **Figure 2**.

(2 marks)

(ii) Complete **Figure 2** to show that 8 million people visited in 1980.

(1 mark)

(iii) Describe and explain what happens at stagnation.

....

....
(2 marks)

(b) (i)   Suggest reasons for the trend in visitor numbers since 1970.

....

....
(2 marks)

(ii) How might visitor numbers be increased?

....
(1 mark)

(c) Explain how and why the tourist facilities may have changed from 1900 to 1960.

> Underlining key words in the question can help you to focus your answer.

....

....

....

....

....
(4 marks)

Unit 2B — Tourism

UK Tourism

3 Study **Figure 3**, which is an extract from a report on a UK National Park.

(a) (i) What was the maximum number of serious traffic accidents involving tourists in any one year?

....
(1 mark)

Figure 3

[Graph showing No. of serious traffic accidents involving tourists (left axis, 0-100) and No. of tourists / millions (right axis, 0-10) by Year from 2000 to 2008. Key: line = accidents, bars = tourists.]

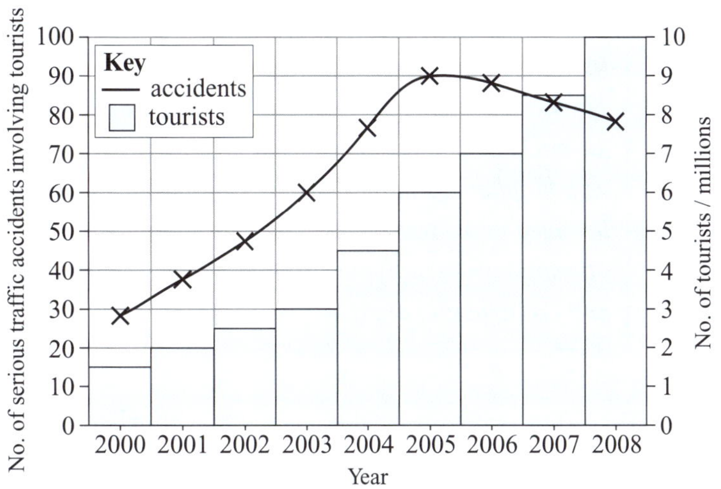

The 40 mph speed limit, introduced in 2005, hasn't put visitors off. Not surprising with all the Park has to offer — acres of moorland and woodland, with over 500 miles of footpaths and plenty of cycle routes. The rivers are open to canoeists in the winter months and they're full of wild brown trout, sea trout and salmon.

(ii) Use **Figure 3** to describe why the National Park is a popular tourist area.

....
....
....
....
....
(2 marks)

(b) (i) Use **Figure 3** to describe the possible negative impacts of the tourists visiting the Park.

....
....
....
(3 marks)

(ii) Use **Figure 3** to describe one way that the Park is managing the negative impact of tourists.

....
(1 mark)

(iii) Suggest two other ways in which the impact of tourists can be managed by National Parks.

....
....
(2 marks)

4 Suggest an action plan for **either** a named UK National Park **or** a named UK coastal resort that will encourage tourists to visit the area.

Choose a case study that you know well, so you can include lots of detail in your answer.

(8 marks)
spelling, punctuation and grammar: 3 marks

5 Describe the management strategies that are used to cope with the impact of tourists in **either** a named UK National Park **or** a named UK coastal resort.

(8 marks)
spelling, punctuation and grammar: 3 marks

Unit 2B — Tourism

Mass Tourism

1 Study **Figure 1**, which gives information about tourism in the Seychelles.

Figure 1

> *The Seychelles is a collection of small islands in the Indian Ocean. Its climate and landscape make it an attractive tourist destination. Thousands of tourists fly to the islands each year, many travelling there for package holidays organised by large travel companies. Its popularity as a holiday destination means that much of the population is directly involved in the tourist industry, working in hotels and restaurants, or offering leisure activities such as water sports. Transportation, fishing and construction are other important sources of employment.*

(a) (i) What is meant by the term 'mass tourism'?

....
(1 mark)

(ii) Use **Figure 1** to describe the positive economic impacts of tourism on the Seychelles.

....

....
(2 marks)

(iii) Give a negative economic impact of tourism on the Seychelles.

....
(1 mark)

(b) Explain how mass tourism might have a negative environmental impact on the Seychelles.

....

....

....
(3 marks)

See if you can pick out info or ideas from the resource for questions like this.

(c) Suggest four strategies that would encourage tourists to continue visiting the Seychelles.

....

....

....

....
(4 marks)

2 Describe the impacts of mass tourism on a named tropical area and explain how any negative impacts are being reduced.

(8 marks)
spelling, punctuation and grammar: 3 marks

Unit 2B — Tourism

Tourism in Extreme Environments

1   Study **Figure 1**, which shows a page from a travel company brochure.

Figure 1

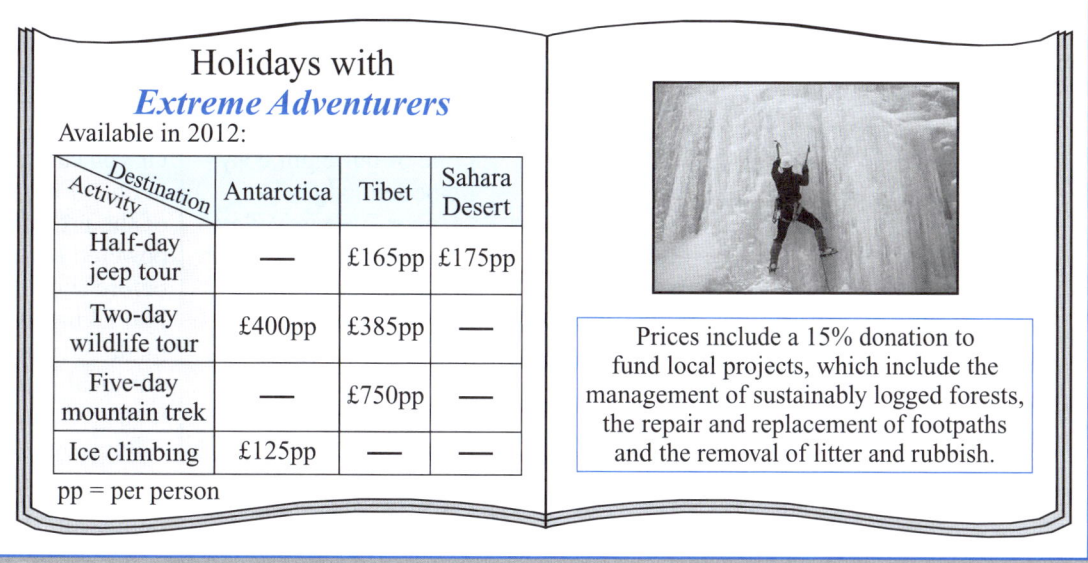

Holidays with Extreme Adventurers
Available in 2012:

Activity \ Destination	Antarctica	Tibet	Sahara Desert
Half-day jeep tour	—	£165pp	£175pp
Two-day wildlife tour	£400pp	£385pp	—
Five-day mountain trek	—	£750pp	—
Ice climbing	£125pp	—	—

pp = per person

Prices include a 15% donation to fund local projects, which include the management of sustainably logged forests, the repair and replacement of footpaths and the removal of litter and rubbish.

(a) (i) Using **Figure 1**, calculate the total price of a wildlife tour in Tibet for three people.

....
(1 mark)

(ii) Describe the reasons why people go on extreme holidays.

....

....

....
(3 marks)

(iii) Suggest why the demand for holidays in extreme environments has increased.

....

....

There are three marks so give three reasons.

....
(3 marks)

(b) Using **Figure 1**, suggest some of the impacts of tourism in extreme environments.

....

....

....
(3 marks)

2   Explain the strategies used in a named extreme environment to help reduce the impacts of tourism.

(8 marks)
spelling, punctuation and grammar: 3 marks

Unit 2B — Tourism

Ecotourism

1 Study **Figure 1**, an advertisement for an ecotourist destination.

(a) (i) What is meant by the term 'ecotourism'?

....

....
(1 mark)

Figure 1

Ingrid's Country Lodgings

Come and stay in one of our eight cosy wooden lodges in Upper Tweedy Valley, home of the wild bears and golden eagles.
 Sample the delights of our locally-produced food and drink, enjoy our hand-made arts and crafts, then dance the night away to one of our local bands. Or you can relax in one of our state-of-the-art, solar-powered hot tubs before snuggling into a king-size bed, made of timber from our local, sustainably managed forests.
 Booking is highly recommended. Call 0131 715723

(ii) Use evidence from **Figure 1** to explain why Ingrid's Country Lodgings is an example of ecotourism.

....

....

....

....

....

....
(4 marks)

(b) (i) Describe the economic benefits of ecotourism.

....

....
(2 marks)

(ii) How can ecotourism benefit the environment?

....

....
(2 marks)

(c) Explain how ecotourism contributes to the sustainable development of the Upper Tweedy Valley.

....

....

....
(3 marks)

2 Choose one ecotourist destination you have studied.

Name of ecotourist destination ....

Describe the ways in which ecotourism has benefited this destination.
(8 marks)
spelling, punctuation and grammar: 3 marks

Unit 2B — Tourism